JUN FAN/JEET KUNE DO
SCIENTIFIC STREETFIGHTING
by
Sifu Lamar M. Davis II

JUN FAN/JEET KUNE DO SCIENTIFIC STREETFIGHTING

by
Sifu Lamar M. Davis II

ISBN: 0-9531766-1-4

HNL PUBLISHING

5918 Fort Hamilton Parkway

Brooklyn

New York-11219-USA

Disclaimer – Neither the author nor the publisher assumes any responsibility in any manner whatsoever for any injury which may occur by reading, following the instructions herein. Consult your physician before following any of the activities.

CONTENTS

ACKNOWLEDGEMENTS

Sifu Lamar M. Davis II would like to thank the following individuals for their participa- tion in the making of this book. Without these individuals this book would not have been possible!

Thanks to Lori Faith Davis for the excellent photography.

Thanks to the following students, listed here in alphabetical order, for assisting in the photographs: Mark Cole, John Drake, Michael McCoy, Harlan McElrath, James Reynolds, Brent Segraves and Phillip Sims. I know this wasn't easy, guys! Great job!

Thanks to all of my students all over the world, for always encouraging me to continue on my path, even through the toughest of times! Without your encouragement, this book would have never been written! Keep Blasting!

ABOUT THE AUTHOR
Sifu Lamar M. Davis II

Sifu Lamar M. Davis has trained in the martial arts for thirty-two years of his life at the time of this book's first printing. Although the first ten years of that was training in other martial arts, he has devoted the last twenty-two years of his life to an exhaustive study of Jun Fan Gung Fu and Jeet Kune Do. These are the fighting methods developed, practiced and taught by the late Bruce Lee during his lifetime. As a result of this, Sifu Davis is now a certified Full Instructor of Jun Fan/Jeet Kune Do, having received certification from three of Bruce Lee's original students.

In late 1988, Sifu Davis started writing articles for various martial arts magazines, first appearing in Black Belt magazine in the March 1989 issue. Since then, he has had over sixty articles published in various martial arts magazines all over the world, and has appeared on the covers of Inside Kung Fu, Inside Karate, Great Britain's Combat magazine and Germany's Kicksider magazine.

Sifu Davis is the Executive Director and Senior Instructor of Jun Fan/Jeet Kune Do Inter-national and the Jun Fan/Jeet Kune Do Trapping Association. Both of these organizations are dedicated to the preservation, promotion and perpetuation of Bruce Lee's original teaching, training and fighting methods and have members worldwide. They also offer an extensive Apprentice Instructor training program for those who want to become instructors of Jun Fan/Jeet Kune Do. For more information on how you may become a member, write to Jun Fan/Jeet Kune Do International, 14310, East 42nd St, Suite B. PMB 372 Indepence, Missouri 64055. They also have an extensive website at http://sifulamar-davis.home.mindspring.com where you can print a membership application and merchandise order forms right off the site.

INTRODUCTION
By Sifu Lamar M. Davis II

Although this book has just been put into print, it has been in the making for a long time! At the time of this writing, I have been an active practitioner in the martial arts for 32 years of my life! I have trained exclusively in Bruce Lee's fighting methods for the last twenty-two years! I have had over sixty articles published in various martial arts magazines around the world. I have completed forty instructional videotapes on Jun Fan/Jeet Kune Do. And now, finally, this book!

For years now, students, family and friends have encouraged me to write a book. What you are about to read is the product of this encouragement! Hopefully, this will be the first of many books, as I have a lot of information to share with the world! For all of those who have waited so long for this, thanks for your encouragement and I hope that you are pleased with the book!

Sincerely,
Sifu Lamar M. Davis 11
Jun Fan/Jeet Kune Do

CHAPTER ONE
What Is Jun Fan/Jeet Kune Do?

Jun Fan/Jeet Kune Do is the term used to describe Bruce Lee's method of martial arts teaching, training and fighting as it existed in his lifetime. Bruce Lee's Chinese name is Lee Jun Fan. Bruce Lee's first school in the United States was located in Seattle, Washington. During the Seattle period, Bruce Lee's art was referred to as Jun Fan Gung Fu. This was a devastatingly Modified form of wing chun gung fu, which Bruce had studied in Hong Kong for five years before coming to the United States. Basically, the term Jun Fan Gung Fu means Bruce Lee's Gung Fu.

Bruce Lee's second school was located in Oakland, California, and his assistant there was a Man named James Yimm Lee. James Lee was already an accomplished martial artist, having trained in many traditional styles of Chinese Gung Fu. During the Oakland period, a challenge match occurred between Bruce Lee and a Chinese man from a different martial arts system. Although Bruce won the fight, he was less than satisfied with his performance! He decided that it was time to make some changes in his system. It was around this time that Jeet Kune Do, the way of the intercepting fist, was born!

Wing chun gung fu still remained the nucleus of the system, but techniques and theories from other fighting arts were added to the formula. Bruce Lee liked the way the fencer quickly and non-telegraphically closed the distance on his opponent. So some footwork, attack and defense theory were taken from fencing. Bruce Lee liked the way that the boxer got his whole body into the punch, moved around lightly and quickly, and successfully evaded incoming punches. So body mechanics, footwork and evasive tactics were taken from boxing. Certain punching techniques such as the hook, shovel hook and upper-cut were also taken from boxing.

Bruce Lee also broadened his kicking arsenal by researching several methods of kicking. He came up with his own unique way of kicking, which was very fast, powerful and direct. There may have been a few more elements, but it is safe to say that Jun Fan/Jeet Kune Do consists primarily of wing chun, fencing, boxing and Bruce Lee's own unique way of kicking.

Bruce Lee's third school was located at 628 College Street, in the Chinatown district of Los Angeles. Here, Jeet Kune Do flourished and continued to develop. This period of Bruce Lee's life and the development of his art is the part of his career with which people are the most familiar, because as he became a more prominent TV and movie star, he got more exposure for himself and his martial art of Jeet Kune Do. It was during this time that he wrote several articles for martial arts magazines and was interviewed extensively through all means of media. He also traveled extensively giving demonstrations of his Jeet Kune Do.

Unfortunately, on July 20th, 1973, the world's greatest martial artist died. After his death his students didn't know which way to turn. Some continued training, some dropped out and disappeared. Some went off on their own to teach and share their knowledge with others. Thankfully, there are several students from each period who are alive and well and teaching Bruce Lee's art. If not for them the knowledge could have been lost forever!

To date, I have personally trained with fifteen of Bruce Lee's original students, each one of whom got something unique from Bruce Lee. Bruce Lee had a tendency to work with each student on what he could do best and hone this aspect of his training to a fine edge. He also had a tendency to use certain students as guinea pigs to sharpen certain special skills of his own Jeet Kune Do. Of course, these students didn't mind this at all because by participating in this, they were also learning it. The point is that each of Bruce Lee's students has something unique and special to offer. If nothing else, maybe just a variation in the delivery of a technique or another way to train a technique!

Learning Bruce Lee's art is like putting together a large puzzle. Each period of development holds important pieces of the puzzle. The more you learn about each period, the more complete your puzzle becomes. My goal has always been to make my puzzle as complete as possible so that I could share my knowledge with others and help perpetuate Bruce Lee's art.

One problem that I see with so many of the Jun Fan/Jeet Kune Do practitioners of today is a lack of knowledge or interest in the wing chun system of Chinese gung fu. I feel that this is another very important piece of the puzzle! After all, Bruce Lee spent five years of his life in Hong Kong training in this method, and it forms the nucleus of the Jun Fan/Jeet Kune Do method. I feel that in order to better understand the roots of Jun Fan/Jeet Kune Do you should spend some serious time researching wing chun and maybe even seek out a good wing chun instructor. Many important elements and attributes of Bruce Lee's personal structure come directly from wing chun!

The reason that we call Bruce Lee's original method Jun Fan/Jeet Kune Do is that one is not complete without the other. You cannot learn just Jun Fan Gung Fu and claim to have full knowledge of Bruce Lee's fighting method. You cannot learn just Jeet Kune Do and claim to have full knowledge of Bruce Lee's fighting method. You have to research and explore Jun Fan Gung Fu and Jeet Kune Do to understand the whole picture. The term Jun Fan/Jeet Kune Do signifies the totality of this learning process.

The three major guidelines of Jun Fan/Jeet Kune Do are: simplicity, directness and a non- classical attitude. Simplicity means that you do what is necessary to accomplish the task in the most efficient means possible without any non-critical motions or actions. Simplicity is not always easy to learn and is often very difficult to perform. Directness means that the attack should take the shortest route to the target without any preparatory, or telegraphic set-up movements.

As Bruce Lee would say, "Use the longest weapon to the nearest target!" Non-classical means that the technique is delivered in a practical, non-traditional manner, with the emphasis being placed on striking the target with the most speed and power. In other words, do damage. Don't worry about whether the technique looked "pretty" or not. Jun Fan/Jeet Kune Do is concerned with effective self defense, not winning forms competitions. That is why it has often been referred to as "scientific streetfighting," thus the title of this book!

This does not, however, mean that anything is Jun Fan/Jeet Kune Do. There is a specific stance. There are specific footwork patterns, strikes, kicks, defensive movements, energy/sensitivity drills, training methods and attack strategies. Some of these topics will be covered later in this book. In a true Jun Fan/Jeet Kune Do class, there are many things that you will and will not see. Below I have listed things that you should not see.

1. Classical uniforms with belts or sashes (Remember the non-classical attitude in training).

2. Barefooted instructors and students (Jun Fan/Jeet Kune Do looks at everything from a practical standpoint; barefoot training isn't very practical).

3. Stiff, low stances with one or both hands on the hip (Jun Fan/Jeet Kune Do has the bai jong, or on-guard, position which is highly mobile and effective for both offense and defense).

4. Striking from a position where the hand is on the hip or drawing the hand back for a strike (Jun Fan/Jeet Kune Do prepares the student to strike from wherever the hand may be, with no telegraphic or preparatory motion).

5. Chambering the leg before delivering a kick (Jun Fan/Jeet Kune Do kicks take the most direct route to the target, using proper footwork, waist and hip action for power).

6. Rigid, classical blocking movements (Jun Fan/Jeet Kune Do prefers the stop hit, or stop kick, using a simultaneous parry if necessary).

7. Kata, kuen or hyung (There are no forms practiced in Jun Fan/Jeet Kune Do).

8. Striking, kicking and defending with the power side to the rear (Jun Fan/Jeet Kune Do prefers to put the power side forward, where it can be most effectively used).

9. Wide, looping or energy-wasting attack and defense movements (Jun Fan/Jeet Kune Do movements are simple, direct and non-classical).

10. Extensive use of the horizontal fist for striking (Jun Fan/Jeet Kune Do punching uses the vertical fist structure for greater efficiency).

11. Use of foreign terminology other than Chinese (except in the "concept" schools where terminology of arts other than Jun Fan/Jeet Kune Do is used).

12. Emphasis on grunting and bowing every time you turn around (Jun Fan/Jeet Kune Do has a salute which is used before and after class, when a student enters class late and before and after a sparring match).

13. Footwork involving wide, sweeping patterns from a low, static stance (Jun Fan/Jeet Kune Do footwork is light, quick and to the point with no telegraphic movement).

14. Non-contact sparring (Jun Fan/Jeet Kune Do prefers contact to prepare students for the reality of the streets).

15. Practicing all techniques by striking the air only (Jun Fan/Jeet Kune Do uses focus gloves, kicking shields, Thai pads, the wing chun wall bag, the wooden dummy, the heavy bag, the double-end bag and other striking apparatus so the student conditions their weapons as they learn to strike with speed, power and accuracy).

There are more things that could be added to the list, but by now you should have a basic idea of things that you should not see in a Jun Fan/Jeet Kune Do class There could be some exceptions to the things on this list, usually depending on whether the practitioner is training in Bruce Lee's original methods or Jeet Kune Do concepts. It mainly depends on the instructor, who they trained under and which period their knowledge comes from (Seattle, Oakland or L.A. China- town).

For more information on legitimate Jun Fan/Jeet Kune Do instruction there are several organizations that you can contact. One is the Jun Fan Jeet Kune Do Association (Nucleus). Their address is: P.O. Box 1390, Clovis, California 93613-1390. The other is Jun Fan/Jeet Kune Do International, 14310, East 42nd St, Suite B. PMB 372 Indepence, Missouri 64055. For more information on training aids and resources, see the last page of this book.

CHAPTER TWO
Jun Fan/Jeet Kune Do Theories

CENTERLINE THEORY

The centerline theory is so important that it is involved in just about every aspect of Jun Fan/ Jeet Kune Do. It is important in attack as well as defense. The idea is to protect your own centerline while you exploit any openings on the opponent's centerline. Most of the body's vital targets lie on or near the centerline.

Right on or near the centerline are all of the targets where someone can strike you and do the most damage. Your eyes, nose, throat, solar plexus and groin are all right on the centerline! Of course the rear centerline consists of the entire spine and the base of the skull, which are also vital targets. The Jun Fan/Jeet Kune Do bai jong, or on-guard position, is designed to offer maximum centerline protective capability while at the same time putting you in prime position to attack any openings on the opponent's centerline.

Also, the closer a blow lands to the centerline, the more impact that gets transferred to the target. This is due to the fact that the strike is landing to the center of your mass. If someone strikes you in the center of your chest, you will be driven back by the impact. If the blow lands on your shoulder, your body will pivot so that part of the force is deflected. This is another reason for protecting the centerline well.

It is important to keep your body angled to the opponent at all times in a fight. If you turn to face them squarely, your centerline becomes more open and it is harder for you to protect it. We do often use the neutral stance for training purposes (the development of rotation striking techniques), but it is not recommended for fighting. The only time that you should expose any or all of your centerline to the opponent is in attack by drawing, which will be covered later.

This photograph illustrates the centerline

THEORY OF FACING

This theory also has a lot to do with the centerline. The theory of facing states that when you face-off to fight an opponent, your position is based on where their centerline is. You should always line up on their centerline. This puts you in prime position to defend your centerline while exploiting any openings on theirs.

To assist you with this, we have what is sometimes referred to as the centerline wall. To get a clear picture of what this is, imagine that your opponent stands about ten feet away from you. Both of you are standing in a neutral, or squarely aligned, position. Now imagine that there is a wall that passes right through your centerline and your opponent's, cutting both of you exactly in half. This wall extends indefinitely in all directions. This is the centerline wall.

Anytime you line up on an opponent to fight, use this wall to achieve the proper position. If you are in a right lead position, place your right foot just to the right of this wall and your left foot just to the left of the wall. Do not get your feet too far from the wall, though, or the groin becomes open as a target. I would say your lead toe should be about 1½ to 3 inches from the wall and your rear heel should be about 1½ to 3 inches from the wall. This gives you a centerline width of three to six inches. Any less than three inches effects the direct delivery of your rear side tools, your torque capability and your side to side balance. Any more than six inches opens up the groin as a target. Your feet should be about one-and-one-half to two shoulder widths apart. This is referred to as your foot width, or stance width. Just face your opponent centerline to centerline using these principles and you'll be right where you should be. This is the theory of facing.

These photographs illustrate three different angles on how you should line up in relation to the opponent's centerline

In this photograph, Sifu Davis demonstrates the proper power side forward position

POWER SIDE FORWARD THEORY

One of the first things that Bruce Lee realized from watching fencers was how quickly they closed the gap to strike their opponent. Part of this was due to the fact that they hold their weapon in their lead hand and move the weapon first when they strike. Bruce Lee decided that if this would work with a weapon, why not with the empty hand!

At that time most martial artist were still putting their power side to the rear, based on the premise that with more travel time before impact, they could hit much harder. The problem there is if it gets to the intended target! With so much distance to travel, it is much easier to see it coming and the opponent has much more time to pick it off with a block or parry! This also allows much more time for a counter attack.

One of the first things that Bruce Lee did with his Jeet Kune Do was to place emphasis on having the power side forward where it can best he used. This cuts the travel distance of the power hand in half. Being that much closer to the target, it makes it much easier to get in with a swift, non-telegraphic lead hand attack. The two most common hand attacks delivered in this manner are the leading finger jab and the leading straight punch. The most common kicking techniques delivered in this manner are the leading side kick, hook kick and straight kick.

Through extensive research, Bruce Lee discovered that by applying proper body mechanics you can get just as much and maybe even more power out of these lead side attacks. This is applying the principle of punching and kicking with the body, not just the arm or leg. There was much skepticism at that time about Bruce Lee's theories. Whenever someone would question this power side forward theory, Bruce Lee would send them to the floor, usually a dozen or so feet away, with his famous "one-inch punch"! This erased all doubt on the spot!

ECONOMY OF MOVEMENT THEORY

This theory states that in attack or defense, there should be just enough movement to accomplish the task. If you move more than necessary, you are telegraphing your movement. Your goal should be to develop non-telegraphic striking ability. In other words, a strike should go directly from the point of delivery to the target with no preparatory motion. This is one of the hardest things for most Jun Fan/Jeet Kune Do practitioners to develop.

Wasted motion occurs in both attack and defense. The most common

In these photographs, you see the incorrect way to move and the correct way to economize structure

telegraphic movements during preparation for an attack are (1) leaning back before moving forward, (2) withdrawing the arm slightly to load up, (3) dropping the body before moving and (4) leaning forward slightly as you start your attack, which we commonly refer to as "falling" into an attack. If you are in the proper bai jong, or on-guard position, you should already be "set" to attack. You shouldn't have to move unnecessarily to prepare to attack.

In defense, you can waste motion by over parrying or by moving the hand in the opposite direction before going to the path of the opponent's attack. Your defense should be based on the kind of attack and the force exerted. You defensive movement should be just enough to deflect the attack off course. If you over-parry, you open yourself up to a quick counterattack from a skilled opponent.

Over-parrying often places you in a prime position for being trapped also! If you pull your hand back to put more force into your defense you could get hit in the process. You can also waste motion on defense by chasing the attack with your defensive movement. It is best to just let the attack come to you and parry at the last instant. This is much more efficient. The important thing is not to get hit! If they miss by half an inch or they miss by three feet, they still missed. It is best to be in range for immediate counterattack!

In these photographs, Sifu Davis demonstrates the longest weapon to nearest target principle using the finger jab to the eyes (left) and the lowline side kick to the knee (right)

LONGEST WEAPON TO NEAREST TARGET

One of the most important principles emphasized by Bruce Lee was using your longest weapon to strike the nearest target. This is basically what interception is all about. In the case of your lower body tools, this would be your leading side kick to the opponent's lead knee. In the case of your upper body tools, this would be your leading finger jab to the opponent's eyes. Bruce Lee himself demonstrated and explained this in the TV series Longstreet, in the "Way of The Intercepting Fist" episode. This was truly a historical moment for all Jun Fan/Jeet Kune Do practitioners, as Bruce Lee was basically playing himself It is like a private lesson with Bruce Lee that you can take over and over again!

This serves really two main purposes. First, it does physical damage to the opponent at the earliest possible moment in the conflict. In the case of the side kick to the knee, destroying the opponent's mobility. In the case of the finger jab to the eyes, destroying the opponent's ability clearly see you and be able to continue to fight. If he can't see you or move to you how can he fight you? That is my point, he can't!

The second thing that occurs is psychological damage. If you attack your opponent at the earliest possible moment and cause them lots of pain, they are going to realize very quickly that they have messed with the wrong person! They are more than likely going to be looking for a way out at that time. If they are able to continue, they will have lost most of their effectiveness if not all of it! I have always taught my students that as soon as they feel that conflict is imminent and there is no way to avoid it, hit hard, hit fast and hit first! Usually the person who lands the first effective blow in the street will be the winner! There are many psychological principles that apply to street situations, but this is easily one of the most important. Remember this!

BROKEN RHYTHM & TIMING

One of the most important areas of your training is the development of timing and rhythm. Once you understand timing and rhythm, then you can break the rhythm on your opponent. This greatly increases your ability to successfully land a deceptive attack on your opponent. This is especially useful to you if the opponent manages to effectively counter your direct and combination attacks! When this happens continuously, you need something to give you the edge!

Cadence is a term used to describe speed regulated to coincide with that of your opponent. You can either follow the opponent's cadence, or you can impose your cadence on them. Usually it is more to your advantage to impose your own cadence on them! Each movement in a cadence is referred to as a tempo. To offset the opponent's timing, you can either increase or decrease the cadence. This greatly effects the opponent's ability to regulate their cadence. Often you can really mess up an opponent who has superior speed just by suddenly slowing downt By the same token, you can also mess up an opponent's timing by suddenly speeding things up!

To use broken rhythm, you start an attack at full speed, pause suddenly, and then continue to your target. This works really well, especially if you have set the opponent up with a series of feints or slower attacks to see what their reaction is! Often the opponent will over-parry, leaving an opening for your strike to land. To be effective with broken rhythm attacks, you must spend many hours working in front of a mirror and with a training partner! You must develop the ability to make the initial movement look real, so that the opponent will give the appropriate response. If you haven't put in the time training for this, I would not recommend attempting it! In the street, you may only get one chance, and you want to make it count! Against an unskilled opponent, you probably won't need it, but it's nice to know that the ability is there if you do!

In these photographs, Sifu Davis demonstrates the use of broken rhythm. From the on guard position (1), Sifu Davis initiates a leading straight punch (2), Mark Cole attempts to parry the punch (3), which Sifu Davis has interrupted. After the missed parry has passed, Sifu Davis continues the punch and scores (4)

THE IMMOVABLE ELBOW THEORY

This theory originally comes from the wing chun gung fu system. According to this theory, the lead elbow should maintain a distance of four to six inches from the lead side ribs at all times when you are in your bai jong (on-guard) position. There are both offensive and defensive reasons for this. Offensively, this positions the lead arm so that it is a little bit closer to the opponent and in prime position for a non-telegraphic strike. It also positions the lead arm for the application of the hammer principle, which will be covered in the next section.

Defensively, this positioning of the elbow offers natural protection for the lead side ribs and solar plexus without even moving the lead arm. This also makes the lead arm free to move both to the inside and outside corners to cover because the elbow is not against the body, which would restrict your lead arm movement. If the lead elbow is out to the side, your ribs and solar plexus are exposed to attack.

Also, the lead elbow is the key to centerline control. If you can control the opponent's lead elbow, the centerline is yours! If the lead elbow is against the body or carried to the outside of the lead side ribs, it is easy to gain control of the centerline. When the lead elbow is against the body, it is in what we refer to as a pre-pinned position. You have actually trapped yourself if you allow this to happen! If you keep the elbow positioned properly, you have the advantage in both attack and defense, and you can't be trapped easily.

This photograph illustrates the proper distance of the elbow from the body

Wing chun gung fu practitioners will move their whole body back to keep from giving away the lead elbow by having it pressed into them, thus the name, immovable elbow. I would suggest that you do the same. It is just that important! Remember – four to six inches in front of the lead side ribs at all times! Also, after attacking, return to this position as quickly as possible.

THE HAMMER PRINCIPLE

The hammer principle is actually quite simple, though not often simple to apply. Most people still telegraph when trying it, even though the idea is to eliminate all telegraphic signs that a strike is on the way. The two most common strikes that this principle is applied to are the leading finger jab and the leading straight punch, both highly effective strikes when properly executed. You just have to really work at it a lot to get it down. Once you've got it down, though, you've really got something!

In explaining how this principle works, I will start from the beginning. Have you ever noticed that when you use a hammer to drive a nail, all or most of your arm movement is from the elbow out? This is what keeps the hammer accurate, right? If you don't believe this, try hammering with the whole arm and you will notice a sudden decrease in accuracy, especially if you hit your thumb! This motion from the elbow out only is where the term "hammer" principle comes from. When applying this principle, the arm movement is basically the same, from the elbow out.

If you are an experience martial artist or boxer, usually when you are in your stance you keep your lead arm moving constantly. This will usually be small circling, rising/falling or weaving motions, right? I'm sure that you also realize that these small motions go a long way toward concealing the initiation of your punch. If the arm is already moving, there is no "start-up" movement for the opponent to see.

Now, this is where the "hammer principle" comes into play. When you are making these small motions, keep your lead elbow in the same spot. In other words, nothing is moving except for the forearm, wrist and hand. Think ofthe immovable elbow theory that was covered in the previous section. The lead elbow is approximately four to six inches in front of the lead side ribs. This is the position where the "hammering" type movement comes from.

Now to execute the strike, drop the lead arm to a level where the forearm is pointing straight at the opponent's nose and let it fly. If done properly, this motion will completely conceal your intentions to strike. This is what is referred to as "dropping the hammer". I witnessed Bob Bremer, who is one of the original L.A. Chinatown students, get in repeatedly on a much younger opponent with this maneuver! And that was after Bob had recently suffered a heart attack! Another thing that has to be considered here is that the opponent knew exactly what Bob was going to do, yet Bob repeatedly got in and touched his forehead with a bil jee before he could do anything about it! This proves the effectiveness of the hammer principle! Of course it also helps that Bob learned it directly from Bruce Lee!

I like to use this analogy. Think of yourself standing on the sidelines watching an archery match. When the archer releases the arrow, you can follow it all the way to the target. Now imagine that same scenario, except for this time you are the target. The arrow would go through your face before you even realized that it had been released! Directness is the key here!

I have also referred to this principle as "aiming the gun" to help my students better understand it. Imagine that the forearm is the barrel of the gun. The fist or finger jab is the bullet. Wherever you aim a gun, the bullet goes, right? If the gun is already aimed, it is ready to fire. I teach my students to "track" the opponent's nose with their lead hand. This greatly simplifies interception! You are like the archer waiting for the proper time to release your arrow! Although it takes much work to get it down, mastery of the hammer principle is well worth the effort! Now you can see why it is such an important part of Jun Fan/Jeet Kune Do strategy!

In these photographs, Sifu Davis illustrates the hammer principle. Sifu Davis moves his hands around to conceal his intentions to strike (1 and 2). Notice that his elbow remains in basically the same position throughout these movements. He then drops the hammer (3) and fires a bil jee (4) in a straight line to the opponent's eyes (5)

RELAX & EXPLODE!

When engaged in combat with an opponent, you should attempt to relax and flow with your movements. Excessive muscular tension will put a braking action on the tendons of the limbs involved in the movement, which will slow you down! Excess tension also causes unnecessary tele-graphic movement, which will give away your intentions to strike.

In some martial arts, the practitioners are taught to make a fist while in their fighting stance and when executing blocking/parrying movements. An open hand moves much faster than a closed fist due to the lack of excess muscular tension. The only time that you should make a fist is just before a punch impacts with it's target. This assures that you are relaxed and can achieve maximum speed before impact. Also, open hand parries are much quicker than closed fist blocks, and require much less physical strength.

Relaxed motion will enable you to deliver strikes with sudden explosive force! If you are already in motion your intentions to strike are concealed by your relaxed movements. This makes it really hard for the opponent to know when you are going to strike. One of the hardest things for me to accomplish is to get new students to relax. Excess tension is a natural trait in beginners. It sounds strange, but you must work to learn to relax.

When you move, there are agonistic and antagonistic muscles involved. The agonistic muscles are those that work to accomplish the task at hand. The antagonistic muscles are the muscles that oppose this task. An example of this is, when you punch, the agonistic muscle that you use to deliver the punch is the triceps. The antagonist is the biceps, yet the biceps is the agonistic muscle for the retraction of the punch. For maximum explosive-ness in your techniques, learn how to best use the muscles to accomplish the task with the least waste of energy.

In these photographs, Sifu Davis relaxes into the on guard position (left), clears his mind and then suddenly explodes into the focus glove with a powerful straight punch (right)

CHAPTER THREE
The Bai Jong Position

The bai jong, or on-guard, position is one of the most important elements to consider in Jun Fan/Jeet Kune Do training. The most important factors in a good fighting stance are mobility and good offensive and defensive positioning. A martial art can be likened to a tree in the way that the stance and the footwork form the roots and the trunk. The offensive and defensive tactics are the major limbs growing off the trunk. All of the variations that are possible from there are the smaller limbs and the leaves. The stronger your roots and trunk, the stronger all of your limbs are going to be!

Working from the ground up, one of the first considerations is the alignment of the feet. There are four possible alignments: square, straight, angular and reverse angular. The type of alignment is based on the position of the fighter's feet in relation to the opponent's centerline, which we discussed in the previous chapter.

In a square alignment, neither foot actually leads. Both feet are an even distance from the opponent. This position offers good balance and upper body mobility from right to left, but suffers somewhat in these areas from front to rear. Balance is easily destroyed by a powerful blow to the front or rear of the body. The fighter will fall unless he can step quickly to recover. One advantage of this position is that all of the body's striking tools are in equal reach of the target. The wing chun style of gung fu makes excellent use of this stance but most fighters lack the skill to make it work.

In a straight alignment, both feet are lined up directly with the opponent's centerline. This position offers good balance and upper body mobility from front to rear, but lacks these qualities left to right. One good quality of the straight alignment is that it limits the target accessibility of your body; the bad thing about this alignment is that you are somewhat restricted to the use of your lead side weapons and most of your torque capability is lost. This is a good stance for tournament fighting use, but most fighters lack the skill to make it effective in the streets.

In an angular alignment, the feet are at an angle in relation to the opponent's centerline. There is a definite lead established here. This position offers good balance and upper body mobility left to right as well as front to rear. The lead side striking tools have easy access to the opponent and the rear weapons also can be easily used. This alignment offers maximum torque capability for either side. Mobility also is greatly enhanced by this alignment. The target accessibility of your body is greatly limited to your opponent because of the angle of the upper body. Taking these factors into consideration, angular alignment seems to be most practical for street use.

Like the angular alignment, reverse angular alignment places the feet at an angle to the opponent's centerline. The difference is that in this alignment the feet are facing away from the opponent. However, offensive and defensive capabilities are severely limited. This position is best used for execution of the spinning backfist and the spinning back kick, neither of which is considered practical for street use because the coccyx, kidneys, spinal column and back of the head are all exposed to attack. The best use of this alignment just might be positioning yourself to run away from your attacker, which is an option that should always be considered!

The width of the stance, or distance between the feet, is the next consideration. There are basically three possible widths: narrow, medium and wide.

Narrow width will be defined as shoulder width or less. This offers good mobility but little stability. The fighter can easily be knocked off balance. If the feet are too close together, a good foot sweep or Thai-style leg kick can take both feet out from under you. This is not a practical foot width for street defense.

Medium width will be defined as approximately shoulder width and a half apart. This offers good mobility and stability. Weight can be easily shifted from one foot to the other for closing the gap, evading or attacking. This is by far the most practical of the three foot widths!

Wide width will be defined as approximately two shoulder widths or more. This offers excellent stability but severely decreases mobility. It is hard to move quickly away from an attack from this position. Use of the legs for attack is also limited, especially the lead leg. This is certainly not practical for street use.

The following photographs illustrate the proper Bai Jong position:

Straight on view of the Bai Jong, lead hand high and lead hand low

Side view of the Bai Jong, lead hand high and lead hand low

Centerline width is the distance between the feet in relation to the centerline. When your opponent is looking at your feet, he should not see more space than approximately six inches between the toe of the lead foot and the heel of the rear foot. Much less than that will effect your stability from side to side; any more than that will make the groin an easy target for a swift kick Three to six inches is the recommended amount of centerline width.

The rear heel will be raised slightly for greater mobility. This makes it easier to close the gap on the opponent in a non-telegraphic manner. By dropping the heel, you can put six or more inches between your face and the attacker's fist, therefore presenting a false distance and allowing more space for evading a swift attack. The raised rear heel also increases reaction speed and torque capability. Pivoting for a kick with the lead leg is easier, therefore the kick is faster.

Front and side view of the foot positioning

The next factor to consider is weight distribution. Some martial artists emphasize stances that place more weight on one leg than the other or standing on just one leg. Such positions can be extremely awkward for offensive as well as defensive movements, and mobility is often severely restricted. Fifty-fifty weight distribution is excellent for movement in all directions, and won't restrict your offensive or defensive capabilities. During the course of a fight, based on what you are doing or preparing to do, the weight distribution may be 60-40 or 55-45, etc. It is reasonable to say that 50-50 weight distribution is the most effective for street use.

Both knees should be slightly bent. The rear knee will be bent a little more than the lead knee due to the raised rear heel. Bent knees give more spring to your position and prepares the body for faster movements. This is also good from a defensive standpoint. It is much harder to break the leg at the knee joint with a kick if the knees are bent. In my school we have a saying: "A straight leg is a broken leg."

The upper body should be erect, not leaning forward or backward. Leaning forward robs you of torque capability and striking extension. Leaning backward robs you of evasive capability and places too much stress on the muscles of the lower back. The abdomen should be flexed

Close-up of the upper body position

and breathing should be light and controlled. The shoulders are lined up with the feet so that the upper body presents a narrow target for the opponent, yet arm movement is not restricted. This alignment of the shoulders is from the heel of the lead foot to the toe of the rear foot.

The arms are positioned so that the elbows are in and down, protecting the ribs, with the lead elbow four to six inches in front of the body at all times. This makes it more difficult for the lead arm to be pinned to the body if your opponent attempts to trap your hands. Be careful not to overextend the lead arm. The overextended lead uncovers the ribs, is easy to trap or immobilize, is easily manoeuvred around by the opponent and takes too much preparation for a lead hand attack. You end up telegraphing the movement.

Both hands should be on or near the centerline so that they offer maximum protection. This also positions them for a straight-line attack to the opponent's centerline with a minimum of preparation. The rear hand is held a few inches below the chin, just to the inside of the lead shoulder. It is the primary defense hand. The lead hand is about a foot or so in front of the rear hand and carried slightly lower, at about solar plexus height. A variation of the on-guard position is to place the lead hand low, about six inches in front of the groin area. It is the primary attack hand. Neither hand is fully open or closed into a fist. This is a very non- telegraphic hand position, where the hands are ready to attack, defend or trap with minimum preparation. Making a fist when it is not needed creates excessive tension in the forearm, putting a braking action on the tendons of the elbow joint, which slows a punch and takes away from it's potential power.

The head should be looking straight toward the opponent's centerline and tilted slightly downward, just enough so that a full fist, vertical or horizontal, cannot get in to strike the throat. The eyes, using peripheral vision, should take in everything from your lead foot to the top of the opponent's head. This way you have a full view of your opponent, as well as constant awareness of your fighting measure.

Your body should be "alive" in light, continuous motion, which greatly increases reaction speed. You can move quicker from a relaxed, constantly moving position than you can from a tense, static position. Remember, unnecessary muscular tension will only slow you down. Relax and explode!

Taking into consideration all of the above-mentioned factors, let's combine the positive elements and see what our stance should look like.

● Foot alignment should be angular (lead foot facing into centerline at a forty-five degree angle, rear foot turned away from the center line at forty-five degree angle or turned slightly more to the front in the case of preparation for the forward lunge)

● Foot width should be medium (approximately 1 1/2 shoulder widths apart)

● Centerline width should be approximately three to six inches, no more, no less (more than six inches of centerline width opens the groin as a target, less than three – poor balance) Rear heel is raised slightly for greater mobility, increased torque capability, to spring load for forward lunge and a presentation of false distance to the opponent Weight distribution is 50-50 (varies depending on the task at hand) Both knees should be slightly bent (rear slightly more than front due to the raised rear heel)

● The upper body should be erect with the abdomen flexed and the shoulders aligned with the feet (no excessive tension in the lower back or abdominal region)

● The elbows are in and down, with the lead elbow carried four to six inches in front of the body at all times (immovable elbow theory) The hands are positioned on the centerline, with neither fully open or fully closed (the non- telegraphic hand) The head is facing the opponent's centerline, tilted slightly downward (just enough so that a full fist, either vertical or horizontal, cannot get in to the throat)

● Using peripheral vision, the eyes take in everything from your lead foot to just above the top of the opponent's head (use proper visual focus principles) The body should be "alive," in light, continuous motion to assist in non-telegraphic attack delivery preparation (what Bruce Lee referred to as "small phasic motion").

CHAPTER FOUR
Visual Focus Principles and Target Selection

VISUAL FOCUS PRINCIPLES

Proper visual focus principles are one of the most essential elements of good martial arts skill. In discussions that I have had with individuals and at various seminars that I have done in various parts of the world the topic of what you should look at when fighting someone often comes up. The three most common answers are the eyes, the hands and the feet. Is it any of these, or is it none of these? Actually, it is none of these.

If you watch their eyes, they can use eye fakes and they can also get you with the "evil eye." What do I mean by eye fakes? They can look several times in a row at a specific target, such as the knee. Once they feel that you realize this they move as if to attack your knee. When you go to defend the knee, they deliver a quick strike to your head. What do I mean by the "evil eye?" This is where your opponent applies some combat psychology on you by glaring at you with an insane look or mean look that gives you the feeling that they are going to rip your head clean off! Of course they can't do this to you if you basically pay no attention to their eyes or their face in general, for that matter.

If you watch their hands, as a general rule, they will usually get you with their feet. Also, it is too easy for a good fighter to feint with one hand and hit with the other, feint a low target and hit a high target, or vise versa. They can also feint a hand attack and then deliver a swift kick to a low line target as you react to their feint. Also, it is too easy to become mesmerized by the opponent's hand movements if you continuously watch the hands.

If you watch their feet, as a general rule, they will usually get you with their hands. If they have convincing lower body feints, they can feint a low line kick and strike your head with their hand. They can also get you concentrating on their footwork and then get you with the hands. If your opponent has single leg multiple kicking capability they can start a kick to one line and attack another as the first line closes. As an example, they could start to execute a low line straight kick and as you react they switch up and get you with a high hook kick.

This photo illustrates the proper field of view using peripheral vision

The proper area to watch when engaged in hand-to-hand combat with someone is their solar plexus region. Using peripheral vision, use the solar plexus as your primary focus point. Why the solar plexus? All kicking movements originate from the hip joints. All hand attacks originate from the shoulders. If you imagine a line going from left shoulder to right hip, and right shoulder to left hip, the lines cross at the solar plexus. This is why it is referred to as your primary focus point.

To keep from concentrating too hard on your primary focus point, you have five secondary focus points, which should constantly be tracked using your peripheral vision. Your five secondary focus points are the head, the left elbow, the right elbow, the left knee and the right knee. If you are constantly aware of these secondary focus points, you may still lack the necessary attributes to avoid getting hit, but their will be no excuse for not knowing what hit you!

This photo shows how the fighter will appear when properly positioned to use the visual focus principles

Why the head? The head is permanently attached to the body. It must go everywhere that the body goes, and since it is the guidance system it usually goes there first. By being aware of where the head is at all times, you know exactly where the opponent is going. Also, tracking the head (more specifically, the nose) is necessary for good interception skills.

Why the elbows? It is physically impossible for someone to punch without moving the elbows. Since the elbow moves slower than the hand, it is easier to watch. By always being aware of the position of the elbows, you know when the opponent is going to strike with the hand and which hand is coming at you. Awareness of the opponent's lead elbow also helps with your ability to trap when necessary. Remember, the lead elbow is the key to controlling the opponent's centerline.

Why the knees? It is physically impossible for someone to kick without moving the knees. Since the knee moves slower than the foot, it is easier to watch. By always being aware of where the knees are, you know when the opponent is going to kick and which foot is coming at you. Tracking the knees is also necessary for good stop kicking and jamming skills.

When engaged in combat with an opponent, you should always be aware of the distance between yourself and your opponent. In order to do this, your head should be tilted down slightly so that using your peripheral vision, you take in everything from the top of the opponent's head to your lead foot. By being able to see your lead foot and the opponent's lead foot, you are constantly aware of the fighting measure, which will be explained in detail in the next chapter.

The mistake that many people make is to look away when they feel that they are about to be hit. You must train yourself to constantly look toward the opponent. If you turn away when someone tries to hit you, you are blinded to what is coming at you. At this point the opponent can destroy you if they are alert! For close in fighting, tilt your head further down so that the chin is not exposed to close range shots like an uppercut or tight hook. Just don't make the mistake of tilting it down so far that you cannot see all of your opponent's available tools.

TARGET SELECTION

This photo shows the primary and secondary visual focus points

Since Jun Fan/Jeet Kune Do is a self-defense art, and not used for sport, all of the prime targets for attack are those that will disable an opponent. There are primary targets and secondary targets. The primary targets are those where the most damage is done immediately. The secondary targets are for when you are following up after a strike to a primary target or when you do not intend to do very much harm to the opponent. Listed below are the primary and secondary targets, rear targets, and the main tools that are most often applied to them.

Finger jab, eyes

Straight kick, groin

Effective long range tool – the side kick to the opponent's knee

PRIMARY TARGETS

● Eyes – Finger Jab
● Throat – Finger Jab, Chop, Half-Knuckle Fist, Elbow Smash
● Groin – Straight Kick, Hook Kick, Inverted Hook Kick, Knee Smash, Horizontal Fist
● Knees – Side Kick, Straight Kick, Back Kick, Cross Stamp Kick, Hook Kick

SECONDARY TARGETS

● Temples – Backfist, Elbow Smash, Headbutt
● Nose – Straight Punch, Backfist, Hook Punch, Palm Smash, Elbow Smash, Headbutt
● Jaw Hinge – Backfist, Hook Punch, Elbow Smash, Headbutt
● Chin – Straight Punch, Palm Smash, Hook Punch, Uppercut, Elbow Smash

Hook kick to the stomach

Hook punch to the jaw

Elbow strike to the face – essential close range fighting tool

Close range tool – headbutt to the nose

● Solar Plexus – Horizontal Fist, Half-Knuckle Fist, Hook Punch, Elbow Smash, Straight Kick, Side Kick, Hook Kick, Inverted Hook Kick, Back Kick, Knee Smash

● Sciatic Nerve – Hook Kick, Inverted Hook Kick, Knee Smash

● Shin – Straight Kick, Side Kick, Back Kick

● Instep – Stamp Kick, Cross Stamp Kick

Knee strike to the kidney

REAR TARGETS

- Base of Skull – Elbow Smash
- Spinal Column – Elbow Smash, Knee Smash
- Kidneys – Hook Punch, Palm Smash, Shovel Hook, Hook Kick, Inverted Hook Kick, Knee Smash
- Coccyx – Straight Kick, Knee Smash
- Back of Knee – Hook Kick, Cross Stamp Kick, Inverted Hook Kick

As you can see from this listing of targets and tools applied to them, Jun Fan/Jeet Kune Do is a highly functional method of self-defense. We do not believe in wasting time or energy when the time comes to defend ourselves. Do maximum damage in minimum time with minimum effort and escape to safety. There are those who would hesitate to attack some of these targets with the methods described, but when your life is in danger you must do whatever is necessary to survive the encounter!

There are more targets and tools that could have been listed, but I confined the list to those that are extremely practical and pertaining immediately to the content of this book. An entire book could be written just on the tools of Jun Fan/Jeet Kune Do and their many applications. In fact, several books could be written on that topic!

CHAPTER FIVE
Footwork and Mobility

One of the most important areas of training in Jun Fan/Jeet Kune Do is footwork and mobility. Although easy to explain in an actual training environment, footwork is not so easily explained in print! So much of the "aliveness" is lost in the translation!

Footwork is so important that is can spell victory or defeat for the fighter! You see, good footwork can put you where you need to be right when you need to be there, or get you out of harm's way when you don't need to be there! Without good footwork, the most powerful tools (punches and kicks) in the world would be totally useless to you. The key here, however, is to move only as much as you need to without wasting motion. Wasted motion is wasted energy! Conserve your energy for the attack!

In order to fully understand footwork, it is necessary to understand range. Good footwork is what allows you to maintain the proper distance between yourself and your opponent at all times. The distance that you wish to maintain when engaged in combat is known as the fighting measure.

THE FIGHTING MEASURE

The fighting measure is defined as the range where you must take a step to reach your opponent with a lead leg side kick to the knee. When you are at this distance, you are what is referred to as "on the rim" of the

These photos illustrate the process of measuring off to find the proper fighting measure. Since this is something that you can't do in a real fight, you must develop the ability to "feel" when the range is correct. Extend your lead leg side kick until it touches your partner's knee when the leg is fully extended (1). Bring your lead foot back down and place it right beside your rear foot (2). Move the rear foot back and assume the basic on guard position (3). Now you are "on the rim" of the fighting measure fighting measure. This is a safe distance to maintain, as it gives you just enough time to react to an attack. If you are further away, you are outside the fighting measure. At this distance you can either do nothing, or you may choose to move around and probe with feints, seeing how your opponent reacts to them. If you move any closer than "on the rim" of the fighting measure, you are inside the fighting measure. Once inside, you should be attacking! At this close range, the first person to move gains the advantage! Let that person be you!

You should constantly work on developing a feel for the fighting measure. Practice with a partner to know right when you are on the rim The "fitting in" or mirror, footwork drill is excellent for this purpose. To do this drill, start by facing off against an opponent in the bai jong position with your power side leading. Start offwith just the push shuffle and the side step. One partner leads and the other partner follows, attempting to "fit in" with their movement. It is as if you are looking in a mirror, as your partner attempts to follow your every movement. The person who is following attempts to maintain a distance where the are on the rim of the fighting measure. Stop and check the distance by having the follower shuffle their rear foot up to their lead, and then extend a lead leg side kick toward the leader's knee. If they can just barely touch it, they maintained the distance correctly. If they can't touch it, they are too far away. If they can touch it, but the knee of the kicking leg is bent, then they were too close. After this process is completed, it is the other partner's turn to lead.

Work on this drill often with a partner. Develop the ability to be right on the rim of the fighting measure every time you stop to measure the distance if you were the follower. Develop "body feel" for this. In other words, you don't have to look to check, you just know you are there! In the early stages of your training in Jun Fan/Jeet Kune Do, try to do this drill daily with a partner if possible. You'll be amazed at what it can do for you!

THE THREE FIGHTING RANGES

Over the past few years, there has been much confusion over the fighting ranges of Jun Fan/Jeet Kune Do! Many instructors have taught for quite sometime now that there are four fighting ranges, defining them as kicking, punching, trapping and grappling. A closer look at all of the notes and writings of the late Bruce Lee will reveal that there are not four ranges, but only three! They are long range, medium range and close range. Kicking, punching, trapping and grappling are actually categories of technique and not true ranges.

Long range is defined as the distance extending from where you cannot contact the opponent at all to where you can reach the opponent

The above photographs illustrate the three fighting ranges of long (a), medium (b) and close (c)

using Bruce Lee's theory of longest weapon to nearest target. At this range, you can use the distance to probe and test the opponent's reactions or you can simply hold your ground and wait for the opportunity to intercept your opponent on their attempted entry. This is normally considered a "safe" distance, as you have time to react to any sudden attacks from the opponent.

Medium range is defined as the distance between longest weapon to nearest target and headbutt, knee and elbow distance. This is considered a "busy" range, as all of the body's natural weapons can be used both singularly and in combination at this range. Most of your trapping tools can also be used effectively at this range. This is a good place to be if you have developed your combination striking skills and evasive tactics. Lin sil die dar (simultaneous defense and attack) movements are also applied with extreme effectiveness at this range.

Close range starts when you can strike your opponent with your knees, elbows and headbutt. These are normally considered "lethal" techniques, as they can and do end most conflicts rather quickly! Close range grappling techniques such as chokes, figure fours and neck cranks can also be effectively applied at this range, as well as sweeps, throws and takedowns. Also, foul tactics such as biting, groin grabs and skin pinching can be used! Close range is definitely somewhere that you don't want to be unless you're the one with the upper hand!

A thorough knowledge of footwork is necessary to really understand the ranges because you have to be able to flow in and out of each range based on the situation and the tools that you wish to apply. For the purposes of this book I am only going to show a few footwork patterns that I feel are necessary to good self defense skills. Mainly the push shuffle, sidestep, pendulum shuffle and the forward lunge.

THE PUSH SHUFFLE

The push shuffle is a linear footwork pattern. It is used to advance toward the opponent or retreat from the opponent. It is very similar to another footwork pattern that we refer to as step and slide. The difference is that with the push shuffle, you actually push with one foot as you step with the other. On the step and slide, you simply raise the foot, allowing the bodyweight to complete the step, then slide the other foot to resume the bai jong position. With the added push, the push shuffle allows you to cover twice the distance of the step and slide, or even more if necessary.

To advance with the push shuffle, raise the lead foot and step forward as you push with the rear foot, then shufffle the rear foot forward to recover the bai jong position. This should be a very smooth, non-telegraphic motion. Watch your head level as you move, making sure that you don't dip down or hop upward as you advance. This is telegraphic, and will let the opponent know that you are coming. Imagine yourself just gliding in toward the opponent, without changing your head level as you do so. Then work to make what you imagined become reality. Such visualization skills are often quite handy during training sessions! If you are striking in conjunction with this forward push shuffle, make sure that the hand moves before the foot. If the foot moves first, it gives away your intention to close the gap with the strike! To retreat with the push shuffle, step backward with your rear foot as you push with the lead. Then shuffle the lead foot back to recover to the bai jong position. Once again, just as with the push shuffle advance, the head should maintain a constant level as you retreat. This pattern is often used to move just out of reach of an opponent's incoming attack.

These photos illustrate the push shuffle advance. From the on guard position (1), push with the rear foot as you step forward with your lead foot (2). After the lead foot touches down, shuffle the rear foot forward to once again assume the on guard position (3)

These photos illustrate the push shuffle retreat. From the on guard position (1), push with the front foot as you step backward with your rear foot (2). After the rear foot touches down, shuffle the lead foot back to once again assume the on guard position (3)

THE SIDESTEP

The sidestep is a lateral footwork pattern. You can either sidestep right or sidestep left. It is most often used to evade an opponent's incoming attack. The most important thing about the sidestep is to get the head out of the way. If you like, for added protection, you make execute a slight covering motion with the rear hand as you sidestep. As a general rule when sidestepping, you will move first the foot closest to the direction that you intend to go. In other words, when sidestepping right, the right foot moves first. When sidestepping left, the left foot moves first You will move the head out of the way of an incoming blow by moving it in a vertical line with the knee of the leg that moves first. The foot that steps second will recover to the proper bai jong position. Although you can sidestep to the inside of an incoming attack, it is recommended that you step to the outside. This puts you in an offensively superior position and limits the use of the opponent's opposite side weaponry

These photos illustrate the sidestep right. From the basic on guard position (1), slip right as you step to the right with your right foot (2). Recover your stance width by immediately moving the left foot over (3)

These photos illustrate the sidestep left. From the basic on guard position (1), slip left as you step to the left with your left foot (2). Recover your stance width by immediately moving the right foot over (3)

THE PENDULUM SHUFFLE

The pendulum shuffle is another linear footwork pattern. You can either pendulum forward or backward. There is also what is known as the full pendulum. The forward pendulum is an offensive movement when applied in combat. The backward pendulum is an evasive movement when applied in combat. The full pendulum is used to evade and immediately return fire!

To execute the forward pendulum, slide the rear foot up to the lead foot, allowing the rear foot to lightly tap the lead foot, then step forward an equal distance with the lead foot. This movement is executed very quickly. The light tap assures that you have covered the maximum distance possible with the pendulum. When training this movement as a drill, you normally just step forward after the tap. When applied in combat, the lead foot goes straight into a kick. This should be a very aggressive, highly explosive movement!

To execute the reverse pendulum, slide the lead foot back to the rear foot, allowing the lead foot to lightly tap the rear foot, then step back an equal distance with the lead foot. This movement is executed very quickly. Once again, the light tap assures that you have covered the maximum distance possible with the pendulum. This movement is going to be executed the same in both training and fighting. It is for evading incoming lowline attacks to the legs. This is the fastest way possible to get the lead leg out of danger!

The full pendulum is used to evade an incoming lowline kick and immediately return a kick of your own. To execute this movement, slide the lead foot back to the rear, let the rear foot swing backward without touching down, then swing back in and replace the lead foot as the lead foot fires a side kick to the shin or knee of the opponent's leg. This "pendulum-like" motion is what gives this footwork pattern its name. The important thing here is not to allow the rear foot to touch down. If it does, the weight settles on it for a moment and it slows the return of the lead leg side kick. You want to catch the opponent with your side kick right as their foot touches down from their missed attempt at kicking you. This makes it impossible for them to get out of the way! This movement should be trained over and over until it becomes extremely swift and smooth. Some practitioners like to execute a highline hand feint as they pendulum backward to occupy the highline and confuse the opponent. This also acts as a counter-balance.

These photos illustrate the forward pendulum shuffle. From the basic on guard position (1), slide the rear foot forward, allowing it to lightly tap the lead foot (2). Then quickly step forward with the lead foot to resume the on guard position (3). This motion would be most often used to close the gap quickly with a lead leg kick

These photos illustrate the rear pendulum shuffle. From the basic on guard position (1), slide the lead foot backward, allowing it to lightly tap the rear foot (2). Then quickly step back with the rear foot to resume the on guard position (3). This motion would most often be used to evade an incoming lowline kick (4)

These photos illustrate the full pendulum. From the basic on guard position (1), as the opponent starts to kick, quickly shuffle the lead foot back to get the leg out of the way (2). The rear leg will swing backward as the lead foot displaces the rear foot. As the rear leg swings back in to displace the lead, fire a direct lowline side kick (3) to the knee of the opponent (4), which should be just touching down from their missed kick! It is a good idea as you do this movement to shoot the lead hand out to occupy the highline and act as a counterbalance for the quick return of your kick

THE FORWARD LUNGE

The forward lunge is the main footwork pattern used for high-speed gap closing. It is very similar to the push shuffle advance, only the push is much harder and the distance covered is greater. This footwork pattern is used in conjunction with an explosive hand attack, usually the bil jee (finger jab) or a variation of the leading straight punch. The important thing here is that nothing moves before the hand. If something else moves first, it gives away your intentions to strike.

To execute the forward lunge, a technique known as "spring loading" occurs. To spring load correctly, shift your bodyweight slightly more onto the rear leg and turn the rear foot so that it faces toward the opponent. With the raised rear heel, this should give you a feeling as if the rear leg is a coiled spring, ready to explode forward when released. This promotes correct ankle alignment for the forward lunge.

From this "spring loaded" position, explode forward toward the opponent, making sure that your hand is the first thing to move. Apply the theory of all positive energy to this movement. In other words, when you decide to explode, all motion should be in the same direction, which is toward the opponent. An example of negative energy would be to withdraw the hand slightly just before the lunge. Other examples would be dropping the body just before lunging or leaning back slightly just before the lunge. These motions are telegraphic, in other words, they give away your intentions before you even accomplish anything! Another method of telegraphing this movement is what is referred to as "falling" into the lunge. This is where your body lurches forward just before you start to strike. This is just another way of basically saying, "Here I come!" With the forward lunge, there should be no "Here I come", only "I am here!" Get it!

Since we have already established that the hand moves first, the next thing is the actual foot movement. As you push offfrom the spring loaded position, the lead foot lifts to a height so that it glides along just offthe surface of the floor. As it touches down the rear foot moves forward swiftly and recovers the distance. Now you should once again be back in the proper bai jong position, having covered two to four feet with the lunge. Based on the length and strength of your legs, a good distance to aim for is three feet! I have known some practitioners who developed the ability to cover four to five feet with a single lunge!

This lunging action should be light and quick! There should be no "stamping" sound as your lead foot touches down. The rear hand should remain on guard during the lunge, prepared to check the opponent's lead hand as the distance is closed or remove any obstructions that the lead, attacking hand may encounter. You should strive to maintain a constant head level as you close the distance. Remember, changes of head level are telegraphic and give away your intentions before anything has actually been accomplished! Once you have closed the distance and you are in, be prepared to follow up immediately with other attacks to finish the opponent off as quickly as possible! This forward lunge is one of the most important skills to have in your arsenal of tools. Work on it often and develop a rapid, powerful close. This one movement should define true explosiveness!

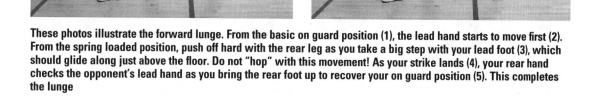

These photos illustrate the forward lunge. From the basic on guard position (1), the lead hand starts to move first (2). From the spring loaded position, push off hard with the rear leg as you take a big step with your lead foot (3), which should glide along just above the floor. Do not "hop" with this movement! As your strike lands (4), your rear hand checks the opponent's lead hand as you bring the rear foot up to recover your on guard position (5). This completes the lunge

There are many other footwork patterns in Jun Fan/Jeet Kune Do, but these are the most important for the application of the material in this book. Work on your footwork until it becomes very smooth and natural. Remember, without good footwork you are "dead in the water" as the saying goes! It has even been said before that the art of fighting is the art of moving. Learn to move well and be able to fight well!

CHAPTER SIX
Defensive Theory

The art of Jun Fan/Jeet Kune Do takes a different approach to defense from most martial arts.

The emphasis is on intercepting the opponent whenever possible. Whenever interception is not possible, lin sil die dar, or simultaneous defense and attack, is the preferred method. In other words, rather than block first, then strike, the Jun Fan/Jeet Kune Do practitioner prefers to defend as they simultaneously deliver an attack of their own. The emphasis here is on the attack!

DEFENSIVE ZONES & PERIMETERS

For defensive purposes, we divide the body up into what is referred to as defensive zones. The area from the top of the head to the solar plexus is referred to as the high hand defense zone. The area from the solar plexus to the groin is referred to as the low hand defense zone. The area from the groin to the feet is referred to as the leg defense zone. As a general rule, any hand attack to the groin is defended with the hands and any leg attack to the groin is defended with the legs. Any attack below the groin will either be stop kicked, jammed, deflected by the leg or evaded. If you reach down with the hands to cover an attack below the groin it opens your head up and brings it in range for an attack. Remember, legs cover legs!

To determine whether defense is absolutely necessary or not, we have what is referred to as defensive perimeters. There is an inner perimeter and an outer perimeter. These perimeters are defined by extending your lead arm fully. The area from the elbow to the body is the inner perimeter. The area from the elbow to the fingertips is the outer perimeter. If an attack comes into the inner perimeter, you have no choice but to counter-attack, defend or evade. If an attack stays in the outer perimeter, you have several choices. You can attack into their attack. You can trap their hand or leg and counter. You can simply ignore it and watch it go by.

THE FOUR CORNERS

If we take the high and low hand defense zone and imagine another line running right down the center of the opponent's body, we have what is referred to as the four corners of hand defense. The two corners closest to the opponent (the lead side) are the outside corners. The two corners farther away are the inside corners. This defines the four corners as outside high corner, outside low corner, inside high corner and inside low corner. Once these four corners are defined and understood, and the specific defensive movements that cover each corner are understood completely, defending the upper body becomes a rather simple matter. All you have to do is read which corner the attack is coming to and respond accordingly with the appropriate defensive movement! It is preferred to defend with the rear hand, leaving the lead hand free to attack!

BASIC PARRIES/BLOCKS

The parry is the preferred defensive movement of the Jun Fan/Jeet Kune Do practitioner. A parry is a defensive movement that deflects the force of an incoming blow, as opposed to a block, which is using your physical force to stop the opponent's physical force. The parry is by far the most economical choice! The block is used only as a last resort by the Jun Fan/Jeet Kune Do fighter.

Specific parrying motions work to cover each of the four corners. Using the rear hand for defense, you cover the outside high corner with woang pak sao, or cross slap hand. To cover the outside low corner, you would use ouy ha pak sao, or outside low slap hand. To cover the inside high corner, you would use either tan sao, palm up hand, or bil sao, which is thrusting hand. To cover the inside low corner, you could use either loy ha pak sao, low inside slap hand, or goang sao, downward circling outer wrist hand. Of course, all of these defensive maneuvers can be performed with the lead hand also if necessary. This is something that you should definitely train! These four corners with the rear hand and the lead hand are what Bruce Lee referred to as the eight basic defensive positions.

The following photos illustrate the four corners of hand defense and the appropriate parry for each corner

Inside high corner

Inside low corner

Outside high corner

Outside low corner

LIN SIL DIE DAR

Defending and attacking simultaneously is what is referred to in Chinese as lin sil die dar. There are several methods of lin sil die dar, but the four corner lin sil die dar movements are the most common. Once again, the preferred method is to defend with the rear hand, leaving the lead hand free to attack. Since the lead hand is closer to the opponent, this is by far the most economical choice.

Lin sil die dar movements can basically occur in three ways. The defensive movement could contact the opponent's attack just before your attack lands. The defensive movement could contact the opponent's attack at the exact moment that your attack lands. Finally, your attack could land just before their attack meets your parry hand. The last is the preferred, as your hit will take most ofthe sting out oftheir intended attack!

The most common hand attacks used for lin sil die dar are the chung chuie (vertical fist punch) and the bil jee (finger jab). Why? Because these attacks offer maximum efficiency in delivery! They go directly from their point of origin to the target. In lin sil die dar, there is no time for wasted movement!

The most common lin sil die dar movements involve defending the four corners! For outside high, the movement is woang pak da (cross slap cover with hit). For outside low, the movement is ouy ha pak da (outside low slap cover with hit). For inside high, you can use either bil da (thrusting hand cover with hit) or tan da (palm up cover with hit). For inside low, you could use either loy ha pak da (inside low slap cover with hit) or goang da (downward circling outer wrist cover with hit). These movements can also be used to defend against direct centerline attacks, although sometimes a slight body angulation is necessary.

The following photos illustrate the four corner lin sil die dar movements

Outside low corner

Inside high corner

Outside high corner

Inside low corner

SLIDING LEVERAGE

Another method of lin sil die dar is sliding leverage striking. Using sliding leverage, your attacking hand is the defense! Sliding leverage is most often used against attacks to your centerline. As the opponent attacks, you fire your attack onto the same line, deflecting theirs off and striking your intended target. It is as if you arm is a knife, slicing into their attacking weapon! Bruce Lee often referred to this method of striking as "cutting into the tool". This could be considered the most efficient form of lin sil die dar. It requires excellent timing, and your striking tools must be well developed. Once again, due to their directness, the chung chuie and the bil jee are the most common sliding leverage strikes. Although sometimes assisted by a check from the rear hand, the lead hand is your primary sliding leverage striking tool!

In this demonstration of a sliding leverage strike, Sifu Davis uses a sliding leverage bil jee to strike the eyes of an opponent who attacked with a punch from an opposite lead

LEG DEFENSE

As we have already stated, the legs are responsible for defending your lower body from the groin to the feet. The most common leg defense tactic is the stop kick, which will be covered in the next chapter. Another leg defense tactic is the lead leg jam. This is where you raise your lead knee and place your lower leg in the path of the opponent's attack. As their attack comes in, you can either jam it or deflect it with your lead leg. Be prepared to follow up immediately with a hand attack. The lead leg jam can be performed either with or without footwork. We have already discussed the rear pendulum, which is used to evade an incoming leg attack. Evasion is the most economical means of leg defense!

Stop kick

A lead leg jam

A rear pendulum

EVASIVE TACTICS

Evasive tactics, the art of simply and economically avoiding an in-coming attack, are an important part of Jun Fan/Jeet Kune Do training. Evasive tactics such as the slip, the duck, the shoulder roll and the bob and weave are all used by the Jun Fan/Jeet Kune Do fighter. Of course we have already mentioned the rear pendulum and the side step, which are evasive footwork patterns.

The slip is an excellent means of evading a straight line punch. The backward slip can be used to evade a hooking type blow. Against a straight line attack, you can either slip to the inside of the attacker's arm or to the outside. The outside is preferred, as a slip to the outside gets you away from their rear hand weaponry. If you slip to the inside, you have to be extra aware of the opponent's rear hand. Be prepared to check it immediately if necessary!

The timing of the slip is an extremely important factor. You want the opponent to just barely miss you, as this puts you in range for immediate counter. If they miss you by half an inch or by three feet, they still missed you! I'd rather they miss by half an inch and me be right in their face before they can do anything about it! If you like, you can cover with the rear hand as you slip Some practitioners feel safer about the slip with this cover, at least in the early stages of training! Covering in this manner still leaves the lead hand free for simultaneous attack.

In these photos Sifu Davis demonstrates the outside slip against an incoming straight punch

In these photos Sifu Davis demonstrates the inside slip against an incoming straight punch

In these photos Sifu Davis demonstrates the backward slip against an incoming hook punch

The backward slip is also sometimes referred to as the snapback. You bend backward from the waist quickly to avoid the attack, thus the term snapback. To get a little more distance with this movement, you can also drop the raised rear heel. Be prepared to snap back forward quickly and counter with an attack of your own!

The duck is performed by bending the knees slightly and dropping the body forward and under the incoming attack to the head. The primary movement is from the waist. The duck enables you to evade the attack and still be in range for an immediate counter. It is most commonly used against hooks and "bar-room brawl" type swings. The duck is not as economical as the slip, but still a necessary part of your evasive skills.

The shoulder roll involves raising your lead shoulder, turning your body inward and burying your chin in your shoulder. The lead arm basically either molds to the lead side of the body or the elbow raises slightly to "bump" the opponent's blow further off target. This movement is most often used against a straight shot such as the jab from an opponent in an opposite lead or a cross from an opponent in a matched lead. It is commonly followed up by immediately firing a cross as a counter-attack.

In these photos Sifu Davis demonstrates the duck against an incoming hook punch

In these photos Sifu Davis demonstrates the shoulder roll against an incoming cross

The bob and weave is used to evade an incoming blow and be in position to counter with a blow of your own as you evade the attack. The motion in the bob comes from bending the knees. The head drops under the incoming attack, and the arms are carried high, prepared to counter as you weave out. Your most common counter attack is the hook punch, and you should train to execute hooks both singly and in combination with the bob and weave. The bob and weave takes much training to master, and should be practiced often.

Evasive tactics are rarely ever used without an immediate counter attack. Practice both hitting and kicking singly and in combination during as well as after evasive motions. Always keep your eyes on your opponent when evading attacks. You should be alert to the opponent immediately trying to follow-up missed blows. If this happens, you certainly don't want to be caught looking down or in the other direction! After all, evade means to make them miss!

In these photos Sifu Davis demonstrates the bob and weave against an incoming hook punch and counters with a lead hook to the body as he weaves out

CHAPTER SEVEN
The Interception

As already mentioned in Chapter Eight, the preferred method of defense in Jun Fan/Jeet Kune Do is the interception. The interception can occur as the opponent prepares to attack. as the opponent initiates their attack or during the execution of the attack. Although Jeet Kune Do means "the way of the intercepting fist", the interception does not have to occur with the fist. This was just one of the many limitations that Bruce Lee discovered in naming a system. The interception can actually occur with any of your tools, hand or foot.

The interception with the hand is most often executed with either the leading straight punch or the leading finger jab. Use your visual focus principles (see Chapter Four) to track the opponent's head. As soon as the opponent is in lunging range, lunge explosively and strike! You can also make use of the hammer principle here, as non-telegraphic delivery is an extremely important factor in the interception. Remember, nothing moves before the hand! As you close the gap to intercept with the lead hand, the rear hand goes straight to check the opponent's lead hand. This assures that you have total control of the opponent when impact occurs!

Of course, you can also intercept with your lead hand without using footwork, but your timing must be excellent, as you will have to allow the opponent to get close enough to hit you. When the opponent comes within range, your lead forearm should be pointed right at their nose. This will enable you to unleash the most non-telegraphic punch possible from your on guard position. You can also push/pivot on the ball of your rear foot and get more body extension to reach the opponent at the earliest possible moment! This is much safer if you intend to strike without footwork, as the opponent will assume that they are not yet close enough for you to strike them! Although the lead straight punch is more powerful, the finger jab offers more extension. Train to execute the finger jab on the most direct path possible with great accuracy, using full extension of the arm to reach the opponent's eyes. If done correctly, they should never see it coming, and they certainly won't see it retract!

An interception with the hand is referred to as a stop hit. When interception occurs with the foot it is referred to as a stop kick. Many practitioners of the martial arts have erroneously identified a stop kick as a kick used to stop a kick. Although this is true, it is just a partial truth. A stop kick can also be executed to the shin or knee of an opponent on their preparation to advance. A stop kick can be executed to the shin, knee or body of an opponent as they initiate their attack, or as they are executing their attack. In other words, a stop kick is a kick that stops anything in progress!

The two major categories of stop kicks are passive and aggressive. A passive stop kick is where you simply raise your foot to the height of the incoming opponent's shin or knee and allow them to run into it. The harder or faster they move, the more it hurts them! You are simply assisting them in hurting themselves! This will most commonly be a side stop kick or a straight stop kick, although any stop kick can be executed in passive mode.

The aggressive stop kick is where you use a kick of your own to forcefully kick inta their leg or body as they advance or forcefully kick into their shin or knee as they attempt to kick you. Against a kick such as a spin kick, your stop kick would be a straight kick to the back of the thigh or buttocks. Against straight line kicks, the most often used stop kicks are the side stop kick (juk jeet tek), the straight stop kick (juk jeet tek) or the oblique stop kick (lin dum tek) Against curved line kicks, the most often used stop kicks are the inside angular stop kick and the outside angular stop kick. Against an opponent advancing from the rear, the back stop kick (hou jeet tek) is often used. The spin back stop kick (juen jeet tek) can also be used to stop an advancing opponent if you have developed the necessary skill to be proficient with it.

To have good stop kicking skill, you must thoroughly understand and be able to use proper visual focus principles (see Chapter Five). The ability to "track" the knees is absolutely necessary for the correct timing and execution of the stop kick. The knees of the opponent will tell you which

These photos show the straight punch being used as the interception tool

leg is kicking, what kind of kick it is and where the kick is going. From there, it's just a simple matter of placing your kick in the path of their knee or shin. They will do the rest of the work for you!

To develop your stop hitting and stop kicking skill, first have a partner fully suit up with the necessary protective gear (headgear, chest protector, cup, hard-style shin and knee guards). You will be wearing some sort of lightweight padded gloves and good shoes such as cross trainers. Have your partner move around you just out of range and suddenly either tele-graph a hand strike, a rapid advance or a kick. You will attempt to track your partner's movements and intercept with the correct timing, stopping them cold in their tracks with either a stop hit or stop kick! Think more in terms of the passive stop kick here, as you don't want to injure your palt-ner. And remember, you'll be up next with the protective gear on!

These photos show the finger jab being used as the interception tool

These photos show the side stop kick being used against a straight kick

These photos show the straight stop kick being used against an advancing opponent

These photos show the oblique stop kick being used against a straight kick

These photos show the inside angular stop kick being used against a roundhouse kick

These photos show the outside angular stop kick being used against a hook kick

These photos demonstrate the back stop kick being used against an incoming opponent

CHAPTER EIGHT
Streetfighting Applications

Everything that you have read in this book so far was leading up to this chapter. Now you will see how the things that you have learned from this book would be applied in a live street encounter. My students and I will be wearing street clothes in these photos, and the scenarios will be many and varied. This is to give you a hardcore, realistic look at how a situation could develop and how you can respond once you have learned the skills taught in this book.

The last chapter will cover what I refer to as vital strategies for street self defense. It is up to you to realize when a situation warrants using the material in this book, and to decide what degree of punishment to issue your attacker! Some situations will require you to reach within yourself and use the "killer instinct" that we all have. Some will require you to realize that there is no serious threat and turn and walk away. Use your head and learn to rely on that "gut instinct" that we all have that seems to let us know whether or not we're really in trouble! Hopefully you will never have to use the material in this book. But if you do, when the time comes, it's best to be prepared!

When that time comes, remember, NO FEAR!

BRUCE LEE'S FIVE WAYS OF ATTACK

The late Bruce Lee, recognized as the greatest martial artist of this century, was well known for being a master combat strategist. He was the originator of some of the most well thought out combat strategies of all time! No literary work on his martial art would be complete without a discussion of Bruce Lee's Five Ways of Attack.

Through his exhaustive research into the ways of hand-to-hand combat, he discovered that there are only five ways that you can attack someone. Every attack in the history of unarmed combat will fall into one of these five categories. They are Single Direct Attack (SDA), Attack By Combination (ABC), Progressive Indirect Attack (PIA), Hand Immobilization Attack (HIA) and Attack By Drawing (ABD).

SINGLE DIRECT ATTACK (SDA) OR SINGLE ANGULATED ATTACK (SAA)

Single Direct Attack is defined as any single attack delivered directly to the intended target witll the intention of scoring. Also in this category is Single Angulated Attack, whicll is a Single Direct Attack combined with body motion or footwork that enables you to strike the intended target from a different angle of delively.

Single Direct Attack is the simplest of the five ways of attack to execute, although not always the simplest to score with. It requires an extremely high level of non-telegraphic striking capability and great speed. For this reason, it is often preceded by a fake or feint to deceive the opponent. The most common Single Direct Attack with the hand would be the leading straight punch or finger jab. The most common Single Direct Attack with the foot would be the leading straight, side or hook kick. The interception would be categorized as a Single Direct Attack, as it exemplifies all of the characteristics of a perfect SDA.

ATTACK BY COMBINATION (ABC)

Attack By Combination is defined as any two or more attacks delivered in direct succession with the intention of scoring. Attack By Combination is probably the most common of the five ways of attack. Good examples of Attack By Combination would be a jab/cross or jab/cross/hook. You can also combine kicks or mix kicks with hand strikes. An example of a kicking combination would be a low straight kick followed immediately by a mid-level hook kick or a low side kick followed by a mid-level side kick. A good foot/hand combination would be a low lead straight kick followed immediately by a lead straight punch to the face or a low lead side kick followed by a lead finger jab to the eyes.

Attack By Combination is probably the most versatile of the five ways of attack. You can combine tools (front/rear, hand/foot, etc.) any way you want. You can use footwork or no footwork. You can combine heights (low, middle & high) any way you want. You can use whatever rhythm you want (strike – strike, strike – pause – strike – strike, strike – strike – strike, strike – strike – pause – strike, etc.). You can use however many strikes you want (two, three, four, five, etc.), with feints or without feints. The combination possibilities are endless!

It is very important for you to work on your Attack By Combination skills. You should work on smooth flowing attacks that progress right from one target to another. Occasionally break up the rhythm and the timing of your attacks for more variety. One extremely important thing to remember is to cover during combinations. When one hand goes out, the other hand covers! When you kick, both hands cover! Always be alert to the possibility of an attempted counter attack from a skilled opponent. Find the hand combinations, foot combinations and inixed hand/ foot combinations that fit you best and work them until they become a part of you!

PROGRESSIVE INDIRECT ATTACK (PIA)

Progressive Indirect Attack requires the most finesse of the five ways of attack. Progressive Indirect Attack involves a combination of attacks, which may or may not be set up with fakes or feints, where the first attack, and maybe not even the second attack is the real attack. Only the final attack is intended to score. The trick here is not to lose the progression. Each movement must progress toward that final target. If at any time during the attack you withdraw, it is no longer progressive indirect attack!

Let's look at this in the form of an example. You are moving around with an opponent. You lunge forward and fire a low-line jab. As your opponent tries to block or parry, you change your line of fire, without withdrawing the hand, and strike him in the face with a backfist. His parry hand is still low w-hen your backfist strikes his face. This is Progressive Indirect Attack.

This time let's start off the same way. You lunge forward and fire the low line jab. Your opponent contacts your hand with his attempted block or parry. You withdraw enough to clear his hand and fire the backfist to strike him in the face. Was this Progressive Indirect Attack? NO! Why? When the opponent touched your hand, causing you to have to withdraw slightly, you lost the progression!

To set up a Progressive Indirect Attack using a feint, you can use one, two or even three feints in preparation. One of my instructors, Sifu Jerry Poteet, who trained with Bruce Lee in the L.A. Chinatown kwoon, taught me a really nice Progressive Indirect Attack preceded by two feints, or three if you count the actual feint used for the PIA. You move in once and fire a low shot. The opponent blocks. You move in a second time and fire the same low line shot. The opponent blocks. You have now built his confidence in his ability to block your strike! As you move in a third time with the same strike, switch up and hit him in the face with a lead hook as he attempts to block the strike. He will be blocking something that is no longer there!

Another interesting way to use Progressive Indirect Attack is to combine kicks. One of my personal favorites is to move in with a low line hook kick, as if to strike the groin. As the opponent attempts to block the kick, I avoid the block and catch him in the head with a high hook kick. The important thing here is not to allow the opponent to contact your leg and don't allow your leg to drop between the first and second kick. The leg should progress constantly upward! This also works well with a low straight kick to mid/high hook kick or a low side kick to mid/high hook kick. Work on these until there is no pause or hesitation whatsoever between the kicks. Just smooth constant progression!

HAND IMMOBILIZATION ATTACK (HIA)

I find that Hand Immobilization Attack is what draws many people to Bruce Lee's art. Most arts have some form of punching, kicking and grappling, but very few have what is known as trapping, especially to the extent that Jun Fan/Jeet Kune Do does! Hand Immobilization Attack involves shutting down the opponent's use of one or both hands long enough to land an effective strike or series of strikes to an open target. You have simple traps, which involve one trap to immobilize while you hit, and compound traps, which involve the use of two or more trapping techniques to clear the line to strike the opponent.

The primary goal of the Jun Fan/Jeet Kune Do fighter is to hit. Trapping is usually the by-product of trying to hit an opponent and having the line obstructed. Trapping enables you to remove or go around that obstruction. If you trap one hand and strike and the opponent uses the free hand to block or parry that strike, then you trap both hands and shut the opponent down completely, leaving yourself with one free hand to blast away with!

You can also force engagement of the opponent's arm for trapping by way of what is referred to as the asking hand. This is used when you run into an opponent who has really fast defensive movements and they tend to parry your attempts at SDA or ABC. The asking hand is thrown at them to draw a response. It is as if you are asking a question, and their defensive manoeuvre is the answer! Although it is not a real intention attack, it must appear to be in order to draw their response. When you use the asking hand you do so in a way that assures a specific response from your opponent. When you get this response, you trap the hand/arm that defends with one hand and strike with your free hand. Remember, you're dealing with an opponent with really quick defense, so your strike must be on the way as you secure the trap! Be prepared for a compound trapping situation if your strike is blocked.

There are those who have tried to say that trapping doesn't work. I find that usually these people have not taken the time or put forth the effort to develop their trapping skills. It is a lot easier to say that something doesn't work when you can't do it than it is to get in there and put in the time necessary to develop the skill! L-A-Z-Y is the worst of all four letter words!

I have found that in order to develop your trapping skills to their maximum level you must have a combination of three different things. They are (l) reference point trapping drills, (2) energy/sensitivity training and (3) mook jong training. The reference point trapping drills teach you the mechanics of trapping. The energy/sensitivity training teaches you to sense the energy of the opponent so that you automatically select the correct trap to fit the moment. Training on the mook jong, or wooden man dummy from the Willg chun gung fu system, puts the po~her into your trapping movements and economizes your structure. This, to me, is the magic formula!

ATTACK BY DRAWING (ABD)

The final of the five ways of attack is Attack By Drawing. Attack By Drawing is perhaps the most dangerous of the five ways of attack. It involves leaving an opening in your defense, in hopes that the opponent will pick up on the opening and attempt to attack. When the opponent attacks, you are prepared to immediately counter.

There are several things that can go wrong with Attack By Drawing. The opponent may not perceive the opening as you hoped they would. You may leave one line open and an unskilled opponent may attack another line. You may be expecting a punch and get a kick. You may be expecting a kick and get a hand strike. Of course the worst kind of Attack By Drawing is when a fighter has gotten lazy and just dropped or lowered their hands. In other words, Attack By Drawing without realizing it!

A good drill to do with a partner is to stand in the bai jong position and practice opening up one of the four corners. As your partner responds to the opening, use the appropriate four corner lin sil die dar movement to counter. To make this more interesting, wear boxing gloves or Jeet Kune Do gloves and actually make contact! Headgear is a good idea for the attacker during this drill!

CONCLUSION

As you can see from this brief description of the five ways of attack, Bruce Lee didn't leave anything out! Each of these five ways of attack can be used alone, or you can combine elements of them to formulate various attack strategies of our own. By training in all of them and having the knowledge of their use, you are a much more prepared, well-rounded fighter.

Sifu Lamar M. Davis II and his opponent face off in unmatched leads (1). Sifu Davis sensing that the opponent is about to attack (2), shuffles forward and intercepts with a leading straight punch to the face (3). This is an example of a single direct attack (SDA) street application

Sifu Davis and his opponent face off in unmatched leads (1). Seeing the lead punch on the way (2), Sifu Davis shufffles forward and intercepts with a lead leg side kick to the midsection (3). This is an example of a single direct attack (SDA) street application

Sifu Lamar M. Davis II and his opponent face off in unmatched leads (1). Sifu Davis senses that the opponent is about to attack, so he shuffles forward (2) into a lead leg side kick to the knee (3). Then, without lowering the leg (4), he fires a reverse hook kick to the jaw (5). This is an example of an attack by combination (ABC) street application

Sifu Lamar M. Davis II and his opponent face off in unmatched leads (1). The opponent attempts a lead jab (2), which Sifu Davis cuts into with a lead straight punch (3). Sifu Davis follows up immediately (4) with a rear straight punch (5). He then traps the opponent's neck and drives an angular knee smash to his midsection (6). Grabbing his arm for control (7). He finishes with a downward angular elbow smash to the base of the skull (8). This is an example of an attack by combination (ABC) street application

Sifu Lamar M. Davis II and his opponent face off in matched leads (1). As the opponent steps in with a lead punch (2), Sifu Davis shuffles forward and delivers a lead hook kick to his midsection (3). As he touches down from the kick, he clears the opponent's hand (4) and fires a punishing left cross to the face (5) and finishes with a rear leg hook kick to the sciatic nerve (6). This is an example of an attack by combination (ABC) street application

Sifu Lamar M. Davis II and his opponent face off in matched leads (1). Sifu Davis initiates the attack by stepping forward with a finger jab (2), which the opponent blocks. Sifu Davis then immediately executes a push shume/pak sao/straight punch combination (3), which the opponent parries with their rear hand. Reacting immediately to the energy of the parry (4), Sifu Davis executes a lin lop sao/backfist combination (5). He then traps the shoulder (6) as he shuffles forward into a knee smash to the groin (7). This is an example of a hand immobilization attack (HIA) street application

Sifu Lamar M. Davis II and his opponent face off in unmatched leads (1). The opponent attacks with a lead punch, which Sifu Davis deflects with a boang sao (2). He then traps the lead arm with a grabbing hand (3) as he fires a hard backfist to the face (4). This is an example of a hand immobilization attack (HIA) street application

*Sifu Lamar M. Davis II and his opponent face off in matched leads (1).
Sifu Davis initiates a lowline strike (2), drawing a defensive response from
the opponent. Sifu Davis has responded by changing his line of attack (3)
and lands a hard backfist to the face (4). This is an example of a
progressive indirect attack (PIA) street application*

Sifu Lamar M. Davis II and his opponent face off in unmatched leads (1). Sifu Davis shumes forward and begins a low line strike (2), which the opponent attempts to block (3). Just before contact can occur, Sifu Davis changes his line of attack (4) and lands a punishing jao sao palm smash to the opponent's jaw hinge (5), following through for maximum effect (6)! With the opponent momentarily stunned (7), Sifu Davis shuffles in and delivers a powerful back kick (8) right into the throat of his opponent (9). This is an example of a progressive indirect attack (PIA) street application

Sifu Lamar M. Davis II and his opponent face off in unmatched leads (1). Sifu Davis pendulums forward into a lowline lead leg hook kick (2), which the opponent attempts to block. Sifu Davis switches attack in midstream (3), avoiding the block, and fires a punishing hook kick to the opponent's head (4). This is an example of a progressive indirect attack (PIA) street application. NOTICE! High kicks would not normally be used in a street situation!

Sifu Lamar M. Davis II and his opponent face off in unmatched leads (1). Sifu Davis raises his hands, exposing his midsection to attack (2). As the opponent takes the bait (3), Sifu Davis responds immediately with a low slap parry (4) and simultaneous straight punch to the face (5). This is an example of an attack by drawing (ABD) street application.
WARNING! Attack by drawing should not be used in the street unless an extremely high level of skill has been developed with this method of attack!

Sifu Lamar M. Davis II and his opponent face off in matched leads (1). Sifu Davis raises his lead arms, exposing his midsection to attack (2). The opponent attempts to execute a straight kick to the midsection (3). Sifu Davis shuffles forward and jams the kick with his lead leg (4) and touches down into a devastating lead straight punch to the nose of the opponent (5). This is an example of an attack by drawing (ABD) street application. WARNING! Attack by drawing should not be used in the street unless an extremely high level of skill has been de- veloped with this method of attack!

Sifu Lamar M. Davis II and his opponent face off in unmatched leads (1). Sifu Davis lowers his hands, attempting to draw an attack from the opponent (2). The opponent responds with a lead straight punch (3), which Sifu Davis counters with a cross slap parry/finger jab combination (4). Sifu Davis then immediately executes a drop step/hammerfist to the groin (5), followed by a reverse angular elbow smash to the throat (6). He then flows right into a reverse side strangle hold (7). This is an example of an attack by drawing (ABD) street application.
WARNING! Attack by drawing should not be used in the street unless an extremely high level of skill has been developed with this method of attack!

OTHER STREET SCENARIOS

This sequence shows another possible response to a right hook. Sifu Davis has assumed the bai jong position (1). As the attacker steps forward with the hook (2) Sifu Davis executes a bob and weave manoeuvre (3) and strikes to the attacker's body with a lead hook as he weaves out (4). He then follows immediately with a left cross to the head of the attacker (5) and finishes with a powerful rear leg hook kick to the attacker's sciatic nerve (6).

This sequence demonstrates a defensive movement against a wide right hook. Sifu Davis faces his opponent squarely (1). As the opponent steps forward and starts to execute the wide hook (2), Sifu Davis lunges forward and intercepts the attack with a leading straight punch (3). As the attacker staggers backward from the impact (4), Sifu Davis lunges forward (5) with a lead side kick to the midsection (6).

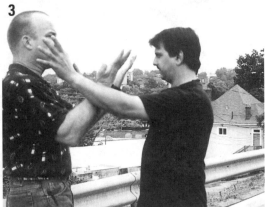

In this sequence, the attacker attempts to grab Sifu Davis with both hands. Sifu Davis faces his attacker (1). As the attacker moves in and attempts to grab Sifu Davis (2) with both hands, Sifu Davis parries both hands outward (3) and immediately executes a double thumb rake to both eyes (4). He then grabs the attackers head (5) and executes a headbutt to the nose (6). He finishes by controlling the head (7) and firing a hard elbow smash into the jaw hinge (8).

5

6

7

8

In this sequence, Sifu Davis faces his opponent in a natural position (1). As the opponent starts to attack (2) Sifu Davis immediately steps in and nails him with a midside kick (3) and follows up with a lead straight punch to the face (4).

This sequence shows a response to a low leading punch. Sifu Davis faces his attacker (1). The attacker steps forward with a leading low straight punch (2). Sifu Davis executes an ouy pak sao (3) as he simultaneously fires a bil jee to the opponent's eyes (4)

This sequence shows a response to a right round kick from the attacker. Sifu Davis faces the attacker (1). As the attacker steps forward with the kick (2), Sifu Davis executes an inside angular stop kick (3). He then shuffles forward (5) and puts the attacker away with a hard sidekick to the midsection (6).

From the bai jong position (1), Sifu Davis steps forward with a lowline straight punch (2) which the opponent parries (3). Sifu Davis immediately executes a pak sao (4) and fires a backfist to the opponent's head, which they parry with their rear hand (5). Sifu Davis immediately slides across and executes an inside pak sao (6) and straight punches their head with his lead hand (7). From there, he steps behind (8) and into position for a rear cradle and breaks the opponent's neck (9).

This sequence demonstrates a defensive movement against a left straight punch to the head. Sifu Davis assumes a right lead bai jong (1). The attacker moves forward with a left straight punch (2). Sifu Davis simultaneously parries the punch with a bil sao and strikes the attacker in the face with a right straight punch (3) and follows up immediately with a left straight punch (4). From there he traps the neck of the attacker and delivers a rear angular knee smash to the rib/solar plexus region (5).

This sequence demonstrates a defensive movement against a right straight punch to the head. Sifu Davis assumes a right lead bai jong (1). The attacker moves forward with a right straight punch (2). Sifu Davis simultaneously parries the punch with a rear hand woang pak sao and strikes the attacker in the face with a lead straight punch (3) and follows up immediately with a rear straight punch (4) and another lead straight punch (5). From here Sifu Davis could continue into the straight blast or just kick the opponent as they fall!

This sequence demonstrates a defensive movement against a right jab/left cross combination to the head. Sifu Davis assumes the right lead bai jong (1). The attacker steps forward with the jab (2) which Sifu Davis parries with a woang pak sao as he simultaneously hits to the face with a straight punch (3). As the cross comes (4) Sifu Davis responds by executing a simultaneous tan sao (5) and straight punch. He then traps both arms with a lan sao (6) and punches to the face with another (7) straight punch.

In this sequence, Sifu Davis is the initiator of the attack. From the bai jong position (1), Sifu Davis fires a lead highline asking hand (2) while stepping toward the opponent. As the opponent responds (3), Sifu Davis traps their arm (4), and shuffles in (5) with a hard leading hook kick to the midsection (6). Still holding the arm, Sifu Davis finishes with a hard rear straight punch to the side of the opponent's head (7).

This sequence shows a response to a left hook. Sifu Davis faces his attacker (1). As the hook comes in, Sifu Davis cuts into the hook with a right bil sao (2) as he simultaneously punches to the attacker's face (3). He then follows immediately (4) with a punishing lead straight punch to the attacker's face (5).

In this sequence, Sifu Davis faces his opponent just outside the fighting measure in a natural stance (1). As the opponent starts to advance (2) Sifu Davis drops back into the bai jong position (3). As the attacker attempts a leading straight punch Sifu Davis executes a woang pak sao with a bil jee to the eyes (4). Sifu Davis immediately follows up with a rear straight punch to the jaw (5), a rear leg hook kick to the sciatic nerve (6) and an elbow smash to the face (7).

In this sequence, Sifu Davis and his opponent start off in mismatched leads (1). As the attacker attempts to deliver a rear leg round kick (2) Sifu Davis stops it cold with an inside angular stop kick (3) and follows up immediately with a leading straight punch to the face (4). It is important for your foot to land just after or right as your fist contacts the opponent's face. This assures that the bodyweight goes into the punch!

In this sequence the opponent attempts to shoot in low on Sifu Davis. The opponent approaches Sifu Davis (1) and starts to lower his position (2). Sifu Davis steps back, grabs his head (3) and fires a hard knee smash right into his face (4).

This sequence starts from close quarters. As the opponent attempts a two handed grab (1), Sifu Davis executes a bil sao with his left arm (2) and a bil jee to the eyes with his right hand (3). From here, he traps the opponent's arm and neck (4) and pulls him into a left lateral elbow smash (5). Sifu Davis follows up by immediately trapping the neck (6) and delivering a vertical knee smash to the face (7) to end the conflict.

This sequence shows a response to a straight kick from the attacker. Sifu Davis faces the attacker (1). As the attacker steps forward with the kick (2), Sifu Davis executes a side stop kick (3) and touches down (4) into a powerful lead straight punch to the attacker's face (5). It is important for the punch to land just before or just as the foot touches down. This assures that the bodyweight goes into the punch!

In this sequence, Sifu Davis and his opponent are in mismatched leads (1).
As the opponent steps forward and attempts a left straight punch (2) Sifu
Davis steps in and deflects it with a sliding leverage bil jee to the eyes (3).
The opponent attempts to deliver a cross (4) which Sifu Davis traps with
an inner pak sao as he fires a rear straight punch to the face (5).

These photos demonstrate the street application of the famous jik chung chuie, the "straight blast". Sifu Davis and his opponent face each other in matched leads (1). Sifu Davis closes the distance with a push shume/asking hand (2). When the opponent responds with a lead hand parry (3) Sifu Davis executes a pak sao/lead straight punch to the face (4). Then using overhand rotation (5), Sifu Davis proceeds to execute the straight blast on the opponent (6, 7 & 8).

Sifu Lamar M. Davis II and his opponent face off in opposite leads (1). As the opponent attempts to fire a rear hook (2), Sifu Davis ducks under it (3) and weaves out, firing a lead hook (4) to the opponent's midsection (5). Sifu Davis follows up immediately with a rear cross (6) and a lead uppercut (7) to the face (8), finishing the opponent off!

Sifu Lamar M. Davis II and his opponent face off in matched leads (1). The opponent steps forward and attempts a lead straight punch (2), which Sifu Davis avoids with a snapback (3). Following his hand back in (4) Sifu Davis nails him in the face with a hard left cross (5) Sifu Davis immediately follows up (6) with a shovel hook to the midsection (7). Sifu Davis flows right into a side neck crank (8) to finish the opponent off (9)!

Sifu Lamar M Davis II and his opponent face off in matched leads (1) The opponent attempts to fire a leading straight punch (2) which Sifu Davis responds to by slipping to the outside of the punch and simultaneously executing a palm smash to the groin (3). From this position, Sifu Davis immediately flows (4) right into a side strangle hold (5) and takes the opponent to the ground (6).

Sifu Lamar M Davis II and his opponent face off in matched leads (1). The opponent shuffles forward and fires a lead leg hook kick (2), which Sifu Davis immediately traps (3) Sifu Davis fires a punishing lead leg straight kick to the opponent's groin (4). He steps down behind the supporting leg as he simultaneously finger jabs the eyes (5).

The opponent falls hard onto the sidewalk (6). Sifu Davis then forcefully slams the trapped leg to the concrete (7, 8). He then drops his knee on the leg, pinning it (9), and checks the arm as he punches to the downed opponent's head (10).

Sifu Lamar M. Davis II and his opponent face off in unmatched leads (1). The opponent steps forward, attempting to fire a right cross (2). Sifu Davis slips to the outside as he simultane- ously finger jabs the eyes (3). The opponent, now temporarily blinded, attempts to deliver a wild left hook (4). Sifu Davis executes a bob and weave, striking with a left hook to the body as he weaves out (5). Now having the complete advantage (6), he fires a hard overhand hook to the opponent's jaw (7), ending the encounter.

Sifu Lamar M. Davis II and his opponent face off in matched leads (1). As the opponent attempts to fire a left cross (2), Sifu Davis intercepts with a straight kick to the midsection (3) and touches down into a leading finger jab to the eyes (4). With the opponent now blinded (5), Sifu Davis shufffles in and finishes him with a straight kick to the groin (6).

BASIC SELF DEFENSE TECHNIQUES

These photos illustrate the extreme simplicity of the bil jee as an interception tool. Sifu Davis approaches his attacker (I). The attacker steps forward and prepares to shoot in (2). Before he can get any further, Sifu Davis fires a lightning quick finger jab to his eyes (3).

Bruce Lee once said, "When someone grabs you, just hit them!" This demonstrates the ultimate in Jun Fan/Jeet Kune Do simplicity. The attacker approaches from the side (1) and grabs Sifu Davis' wrist (2). Sifu Davis responds immediately by immediately by just punching him full in the face (3). He then traps his shoulder (5) and fires a hard straight shin smash into his groin.

In this sequence, Sifu Davis is attacked from behind. Sifu Davis is walking along as an attacker approaches from the rear (1). Sifu Davis picks this up with his peripheral vision and turns to see the attacker almost on him (2). Sifu Davis responds quickly with a hard back stop kick to the attacker's midsection (3) and an immediate qua chuie to the attacker's face (4). The qua chuie is followed immediately (5) by a hard cross to the jaw hinge (6) to finish the conflict.

In this sequence, Sifu Davis is attacked from the rear. Sifu Davis picks up an attacker coming in from the rear with his peripheral vision (1). He turns to see the attacker (2) and executes a hard back kick (3) to the attacker's solar plexus (4). Sifu Davis touches down from the kick (5) and positions himself (6) for a knee smash to the attacker's head (7) and a cross stamp to the opponent's foot (8). He then ties the opponents arm up with a reverse figure four armlock and drives his face into the bricks (9).

In this sequence, Sifu Davis is leaning on a wall (1). An attacker attempts to pin him to the wall and strike him (2). Before the attacker can get off his punch, Sifu Davis executes a simultaneous bil jee/straight kick (3) to the attacker's eyes/groin (4) and follows up immediately by slamming (5) the attacker face first into the wall (6) and then into the sidewalk (7). Notice how the arm and hair are used for control here.

These photos demonstrate how the back kick can be used as an interception tool. Sifu Davis notices an opponent approaching from the rear (1). He takes one more step forward as he turns to face the attacker (2). He then explodes (3) into a powerful back kick to the opponent's midsection (4).

Sifu Davis assumes a right lead bai jong against a knife wielding opponent (1). As Sifu Davis moves in the attacker swings (2) with a lateral slashing motion aimed at the face, which he evades with a backward slip (3) as he fires a hard lead hook kick into the opponent's groin (4).

In this sequence, Sifu Davis is attacked by a knife wielding opponent. Sifu Davis stands facing the opponent (1). As the opponent steps forward and starts his thrust (2), Sifu Davis angles to the outside of the arm and parries the thrust (3) as he simultaneously finger jabs the eyes of the attacker (4). He then parries the knife arm away (5) as he kicks to the attacker's knee (6).

4

5

6

As Sifu Davis emerges from an underground walkway (1) he notices a stick wielding opponent preparing to attack (2). As the attacker swings with a forehand strike (3) Sifu Davis executes a simultaneous bil sao and lead straight punch to the face (4). Sifu Davis then checks the arm and fires a rear straight punch to the attacker's face (5) and a vertical knee smash to his midsection (6).

Sifu Davis is attacked by a stick wielding opponent. Sifu Davis faces his opponent (1). As the opponent attacks with a forehand swing (2), Sifu Davis evades the stick (3). As the attacker attempts to follow up with a backhand swing (4), Sifu Davis immediately returns forward (5) and stops the swing with a bil sao as he punches the attacker in the face (6). He follows up with an armbar to disarm the attacker (7) as he fires a knee smash to the shoulder (8).

5

6

8

7

As Sifu Davis emerges from an underground walkway (1) he is attacked by a stick wielding opponent (2). As the opponent delivers a backhand swing, Sifu Davis executes a left palm stop to his elbow (3) and fires a hard right straight punch to his nose (4) and straight kick to his groin (5). From there, Sifu Davis traps his arm (6) and fires a hard lateral elbow smash right into his jaw (7).

In this sequence Sifu Davis is attacked by two opponents. Sifu Davis faces off against his opponents (1). As the first attacker comes in (2) Sifu Davis intercepts his attack with a leading side stop kick to the knee (3) and a straight punch to the face (4). As the second attacker swings with a hook (5), Sifu Davis responds immediately with a bil sao/lead straight punch (6) and a straight kick to the groin (7). He then grabs his hair (8) and knee smashes him in the face (9).

5

6

7

8

9

2

3

1

4

5

6

7

8

9

In this sequence Sifu Davis is attacked by three opponents. Sifu Davis faces off against his opponents (1). As the first one comes in (2), Sifu Davis lunges at him and finger jabs his eyes (3). He then grabs him (4) and shoves him into the second attacker (5). He then kicks the third attacker in the groin (6) and follows up with a straight kick to his face (7). As the second attacker comes in (8) he catches a side kick right in the solar plexus (9).

CHAPTER NINE
Vital Strategies for Street Self Defense

Self-defense in the street is a serious matter. You must be able to justify the force that you use to defend yourself. Try to get by with using as little force as possible to eliminate the threat. Different countries and different states have various laws that determine what is considered justifiable or necessary force in a self-defense situation. If you are an actively training martial arts practitioner and you intend to use your skills if necessary, it would be wise to check with the laws in your area so that you will be aware of what you could be facing should you ever have to go to court.

Following are some street combat strategies that I have learned in the past thirty-two years of training in the martial arts. All of them fit within the framework of Bruce Lee's Jeet Kune Do, and should be applied using the techniques shown in this book. Read these strategies carefully, learn them and apply them. The just might save your life or enable you to save someone else's!

THE STRATEGIES

● When your life is threatened, you must be ruthless. There is no Mr. Nice Guy in a situation like this.

● Do not inflict any more damage to an attacker than what is necessary to end the conflict and allow you to safely escape.

● Make yourself fully proficient with a wide variety of tools at long, medium and close range.

● Use proper visual focus principles.

● Attack vital targets (the eyes, nose, throat, solar plexus, groin, sciatic nerve, knee and shin) immediately.

● Hit fast, hit hard and hit first. As soon as you know that conflict is imminent and inevitable, take your opponent out.

● Your opponent can't hit what he can't see. Strike his eyes with a finger jab.

● Destroy the foundation and the upper body dies, too. Kick the knee, shin or sciatic nerve to disable your attacker's support system.

● Intercept incoming attacks at the earliest possible moment. As soon as your opponent is in range, hit him.

● Use the longest weapon to strike the nearest target. For example, deliver a side kick to the knee.

● Employ simultaneous defense and attack techniques. Rather than blocking and then attacking, parry or block and strike at the same time.

● Defend your upper body with your hands and your lower body with your legs. Do not bend down to parry or block a kick and leave your head open for attack.

● An opponent can't hit what he can't reach. Use fluid footwork to evade attacks and control the range. Try to stay just on the rim of the fighting measure when moving or preparing your attack.

● Use combinations. In self-defense situations, conflicts are rarely ever ended with just one blow. Be prepared to follow up with attacks until the opponent is down and out.

● If someone grabs you, hit them. Remember: simplicity. No wasted time, no wasted motion

● At close range, use your infighting tools such as headbutts, elbows and knees.

● If your opponent has a knife, prepare for the possibility of being cut. Chances are that it will happen, so be psychologically prepared for it so you don't just lose control.

● Don't go to the ground. Your opponent may have friends waiting to help him.

● When in doubt, throw a straight blast. This is the fastest repetition punching method possible.

● Be prepared to kick him when he is down. Don't give him the chance to get up and come after you.

● Get it over with. There is no time to play around. Take the attacker out as quickly as possible. Extra time offers too many possibilities for error, such as friends to help them out, access to weaponry or an injury to a friend, loved one or innocent bystander.

● When it's over, get out of there. Don't stay around for photos and autographs.

● Do not go looking for trouble, but always be aware that it is out there. Unfortunately, there are those who thrive on causing pain and creating fear in others. Being aware that they are out there causes you to be constantly alert and aware, ready for whatever may come.

● Do not smoke, drink or use drugs of an illegal nature. An alert mind and fit body will be to your advantage in a street conflict. I have always taught my students this: If you take care of your body it will take care of you. If you let it down it will let you down. It's just that simple.

● If you should encounter police or other law enforcement officials be totally cooperative with them. Depending on the severity of the damage done to your attacker(s), you may want to immediately secure an attorney. The first words out of your mouth should be, "I was in fear for my life!"

● The bottom line is this: It's always better to be tried by twelve than carried by six!

RECOMMENDED RESOURCES

Organizations

Jun Fan/Jeet Kune Do International
14310 East 42nd Street, Suite B,
PMB Indepence, Missouri 64055
http://sifulamardavis.home.mindspring.com

Jun Fan/Jeet Kune Do Trapping Association
14310 East 42nd Street, Suite B,
PMB Indepence, Missouri 64055
http://sifulamardavis.home.mindspring.com

Jun Fan Jeet Kune Do
P. 0. Box 1390
Clovis, CA 93613-1390
http://www.jkd.com

Books & Periodicals

Bruce Lee Library Series
Charles E. Tuttle Co., lnc.
RR I Box 231-5
North Clarendon, VT 05759

BRUCE LEE Magazine
C. F. W. Enterprises
4201 Vanowen Place
Burbank, CA 91505

Jeet Kune Do Kickboxing by Chris Kent & Tim Tackett

Jun Fan/Jeet Kune Do Textbook by Chris Kent & Tim Tackett

Above Two Books Available From:
Unique Publications
4201 Vanowen Place
Burbank, CA 91505

Tao of Jeet Kune Do by Bruce Lee

Bruce Lee's Fighting Methods by Bruce Lee & Mito Uyehara
    Volume 1: Self-Defense Techniques
    Volume 2: Basic Training
    Volume 3: Skill in Techniques
    Volume 4: Advanced Techniques

Chinese Gung Fu: The Philosophical Art of Self Defense by Bruce Lee

The Bruce Lee Story by Linda Lee Cadwell

Bruce Lee: The Incomparable Fighter by Mito Uyehara

Wing Chun Kung Fu / Jeet Kune Do: A Comparison, Volume 1 by William Cheung & Ted Wong

All of The Above Books Are Available From:
Ohara Publications, Inc.
24715 Ave. Rockefeller
P. 0. Box 918
Santa Clarita, CA 91380-9018

Bruce Lee: Between Wing Chun & Jeet Kune Do by Jesse Glover

Bruce Lee's Non-Classical Gung Fu by Jesse Glover

New Non-Classical Gung Fu by Jesse Glover

Above Books Available From:
Jesse R. Glover
P.O.Box21745
Seattle, WA 98111

Remembering Bruce by James Bishop
(Available Soon)

Instructional Videotapes
Jun Fan/Jeet Kune Do Complete by Sifu Lamar M. Davis II
(Twenty Volume Series)

Real Jun Fan/Jeet Kune Do by Sifu Lamar M. Davis Il

Jun Fan/Jeet Kune Do Seminar Series by Sifu Lamar M. Davis 11
(Fifteen Volume Series)

The Above Videos Are Available From:
Sifu Lamar M. Davis II
14310 East 42nd Street, Suite B, PMB 372 Indepence, Missouri 64055
http://sifulamardavis.home.mindspring.com
sifulamardavis@mindspring.com

Jeet Kune Do by Jerry Poteet

(Six Volume Set)

Available From:
I & I Sports
19751 S. Figueroa Street
Carson, CA 90745

Dynamic Jeet Kune Do by Chris Kent
(Four Volume Set)

Available From:
Chris Kent
P. 0. Box 16262
Boise, Idaho 83 715-6262